THE
DRY BAR

Published in 2024 by OH! Life
An imprint of Welbeck Non-Fiction Limited, part of Welbeck Publishing
Group. Offices in London, 20 Mortimer Street, London W1T 3JW, and
Sydney, Level 17, 207 Kent Street, Sydney NSW 2000 Australia.
www.welbeckpublishing.com

A CIP catalogue record for this book is available from the British Library.

ISBN 978-1-83861-209-2

Publisher: Lisa Dyer
Copy editor: Theresa Bebbington
Production: Jess Brisley
Printed and bound in China

10 9 8 7 6 5 4 3 2 1

THE
DRY BAR

60 RECIPES FOR
ZERO-PROOF CRAFT COCKTAILS

OWEN WILLIAMS

CONTENTS

INTRODUCTION

Although I'd spent many years making cocktails, it wasn't until my wife, Mari, was pregnant with our son, Tomi, during the first lockdown in 2020 that I delved into the world of non-alcoholic cocktails. Before this, I had found it difficult to create non-alcoholic cocktails that achieved the same depth of flavour as the classic cocktails I loved – mostly due to the lack of products available. However, in the last few years there has been a surge of fantastic alcohol-free spirits, sparkling wines and other alternatives. Creating 'virgin' cocktails is now easier, more accessible and more delicious than ever before.

Many 'zero-proof' spirits are created using the same distillation process as alcoholic spirits, which gives you access to the same incredible flavours. It also allows cocktail-makers to create non-alcoholic versions that don't compromise on the end result.

As demand for non-alcoholic drinks continues to increase – whether it's Dry January, for designated drivers or just those wanting to enjoy a 'proper' drink without the downsides – this book offers you the chance to enjoy the classic flavours and techniques of cocktail-making without the use of alcohol. I hope it will give you the opportunity to have fun creating many different varieties and styles of cocktails at home.

My ethos with all cocktails is to start with a classic recipe – after all, they are classics for a reason. From there, I enjoy giving them a little twist while keeping the fundamental flavours, to ensure I'm bringing the best out of the cocktail and the accompanying non-alcoholic spirit I'm using. This could be adding fresh grapefruit juice to enhance the bittersweet flavour of an aperitif, or adding a rosemary syrup to a botanical spirit that has herbaceous flavours.

I wanted to create a book that would give you exciting non-alcoholic recipes to create and enjoy at home and that you could use for entertaining, impressing your guests with the beautiful fresh flavours and garnishes. And I hope the following pages give you the confidence to try putting your own twist on drinks, and the inspiration to create your own cocktails to enjoy and share.

OWEN WILLIAMS

DRY BAR ESSENTIALS

This book aims to treat the 'mocktail' like the carefully crafted cocktail it can (and should) be, with regard to the ingredients, mixology and the same cocktail experience . . . but without the negative effects that often come from alcohol.

Here you will discover the basics what you need to know about cocktail equipment and glassware; the key equipment is exactly the same for non-alcoholic cocktails as for alcoholic ones. As well as exploring the importance of different glassware for specific cocktails, we'll also look at garnishes. The garnish is an important part of a cocktail as it adds to both the aesthetic and the taste, which will help take your cocktail to the next level. So, here are some of the essentials you will need on your cocktail journey.

EQUIPMENT

SHAKER
The key piece of equipment you'll need is the cocktail shaker. This can come in a few different forms, including the Boston, Cobbler and Parisian. All three create a sealed container in which you can mix the ingredients with ice, and chill the drink quickly. Although there are differences between them, for the purposes of this book any style of mixer will work.

MIXING GLASS
As opposed to the shaker above, a mixing glass is for those cocktails that should be stirred, not shaken. Although you could stir in the shaker, the weighted bottom and straight sides of a mixing glass make doing so a lot easier.

BARSPOON
The barspoon has multiple uses when making cocktails, whether adding an ingredient, measuring or stirring a cocktail in the cocktail glass. Another function is to stir a built cocktail to ensure it has been mixed equally.

STRAINERS AND SIEVE
It is vitally important when shaking or stirring cocktails that they are strained, to ensure the correct dilution and balance. When a cocktail has been shaken, it requires double straining with a Hawthorne strainer and sieve. This is to ensure that all the ice shards are removed so the cocktail is not diluted. When the cocktail is stirred, only a single strain is required and a Julep strainer is the recommended choice.

MUDDLER
The muddler is a key piece of equipment used to extract the juice and oils from fruit to increase the depth of flavour – for example the lime in a Mojito (see pages 70, 76 and 82).

JIGGER
Free-pouring alcoholic spirits is rarely a good idea, but even with non-alcoholic spirits it can completely ruin the balance of your drink and allow the spirit to overpower any other flavour. That's why a jigger is always essential. Typically metal and double-ended, with a single and double shot measure, jiggers allow you to measure liquid ingredients accurately.

JUICER
There are several ways to juice your fruit for a cocktail, with the key objective being to extract as much juice as possible from the fruit. With citrus being a key ingredient in many cocktails, it is imperative that you can juice quickly and use as much of the fruit as possible. My preferred option is a Mexican elbow citrus squeezer, due to its design and how quick and efficient it is.

GLASSWARE

CHAMPAGNE COUPE

The Champagne coupe is a fantastic, versatile entertaining glass, and it's usually used (as the name suggests) for Champagne or sparkling wine. It is also a great cocktail glass, popular for the modern-day classic the Espresso Martini (see page 142) and ideal for my Raspberry & Thyme Bellini (see page 24). There are several stories about the origins of the bowl-shaped glass, most famously that the coupe was designed for Marie Antoinette and was modelled on her left breast. Another is that Napoleon had the design commissioned after Empress Josephine's breast. Whatever the origin, it became popular in the 1920s and is now almost symbolic of the era – just think of Leonardo DiCaprio in *The Great Gatsby*.

FLUTE

The Champagne flute was developed back in the early 1800s and has now become the most popular glass for Champagne and other sparkling wines. One reason is that its narrow design allows the wine to keep its fizz and aroma for longer. Flutes have also been used for cocktails for hundreds of years, including popular classics such as the French 75 (or my Melon & Honey 75, see page 36).

WINE GLASS

In addition to the obvious use, wine glasses have become more and more popular in the cocktail world. With the Aperol Spritz becoming a phenomenon across the world, and cocktails such as Hugo's Driving (see page 26) increasing in popularity, wine-glass cocktails are appearing on more bar menus.

JUG (PITCHER)

I have added a Party Cocktail, which serves 8–10 people, to each section of the book. Served in a jug, the idea is to have a cocktail with the same delicious flavour and intensity of a single serve but made to be enjoyed by the collective – perfect for welcome drinks.

ROCKS (OLD-FASHIONED)

The rocks glass is one of the most common cocktail glasses in the world and is used for some of the most popular – and, in my opinion, best – drinks, such as the Negroni (see my Nogroni on page 110). Its design allows for versatility, being able to hold a cocktail over ice or one poured all the way to the rim, as you would with a sour.

HIGHBALL OR COLLINS

Another common glass, and a must behind any cocktail bar, is the highball. It is the classic mixer glass and can be used for many cocktails. The glass allows all the ingredients to be seen clearly, such as in the Strawberry & Basil Tonic (see page 40), where you see the distribution of fruit and basil. The highball is also a fantastic glass for float cocktails, such as a classic Dark & Stormy, as again you can see the layers very distinctly.

MARTINI

The Martini glass was introduced in Paris in 1925 as a modern take on the coupe. Shaped like a small, inverted triangle on a wine-glass stem, it is the glass that many people visualize when talking about cocktails and was made famous through classics such as the gin Martini and the Manhattan.

BAR KNOW-HOW

The key to creating cocktails is achieving a great flavour, and you can only achieve this through balance. It is important to think carefully about flavour combinations that work well together; you don't want one flavour overpowering another. Each ingredient should complement the others. When using sour flavours such as citrus, there is a need for sweetness to ensure a well-balanced serve. This can also be said for the balance between bitter and sweet, which is found in cocktails in the Bittersweet chapter (see pages 102–15).

To create a stand-out cocktail, you obviously need it to taste great, but you must also consider the aesthetic of the serve. Rich colour and consistency are incredibly important. Egg white tops on sour cocktails or distinct layers can create real impact, but it doesn't have to be complicated, and small touches can make a big difference. Consider, for instance, putting your garnish on one side, and think about which glass will create the most appealing appearance.

MUDDLING

When creating a shaken cocktail with fruit, muddle first to ensure that as much juice and flavour as possible are extracted. This helps in the shaking process to combine the ingredients effectively. To muddle, simply put the fruit and herbs in the bottom of the mixing glass or shaker and pound with the muddler.

PREPPING

When preparing cocktails, a consistent appearance is imperative for the best results. When you are entertaining guests, try to prepare ingredients such as syrups, fruit, ice, etc. beforehand. This will allow you to create the cocktails more quickly and will look more impressive; it will also allow you to enjoy yourself instead of being confined to your home cocktail station!

SHAKING & STIRRING

Someone's shaking technique can be personal to them, but the key outcome must be the same: to chill your cocktail and dilute it by the right amount to ensure the balance of the serve. A mixing glass and the stirring method should always be used with clear ingredients, as shaking creates a cloudy effect and you'll lose the clarity of the liquid.

TEMPERATURES & ICE

The two types of ice referred to in the book are cubed and crushed, and these should be filled to the top of the mixing glass to give the ice less room to melt and dilute your drink. It is important to keep the temperature of the drink as low as possible. Chilling your glass can help this process. When using Champagne coupes or Martini glasses, fill them with crushed ice when preparing the cocktail, then remove before you add the cocktail. You can store glasses in the freezer for the same effect.

EGG WHITE

Egg whites are found in many different cocktail recipes and are a fantastic ingredient to help add a creamy texture. The foam is so pleasing when taking your first sip. Maybe most famously found in an Amaretto Sour, Whisky Sour and Gin Fizz, I've used it in my Grapefruit & Rosemary Sour (see page 108) and Blood Orange Fizz (see page 112), among others.

It is important when separating the egg white from the egg yolk that you use a different glass to avoid any chance of the yolk or shell getting into your drink. When using egg white or other foamers, first shake it without ice to combine the ingredients and create the frothy texture. Then add ice and shake again to chill.

HERBOLOGY

As you work your way through the recipes in this book, you will see that herbs are often featured. They add a fresh, flavoursome attribute to a cocktail and help enhance other ingredients. They also help extend and elevate the taste. Herbs make for a great garnish because they usually have an intense, prominent aroma. When using a herb garnish, clap it in your hands first to help release its bouquet.

CITRUS & OTHER FRUITS

Citrus fruits are important and popular in cocktails, for both acidity and balance, and it is key that we extract as much flavour as possible. Before cutting and juicing a lemon or lime, roll it on a surface, using the palm of your hand with force, to soften the flesh and help extract more juice. It is also important to measure the fresh juice for consistency, so in the recipe I have, for example, stipulated 30 ml (1 fl oz) of lime juice instead of the juice from one lime.

Another element that is added to some cocktails is the oil from some fruit, expressed over the top of the cocktail. This adds the fruit's intense flavour and strong aroma to the

cocktail. To express orange oil from the peel, fold the peel in half, with the white pith facing you, then hold it above the glass and exert pressure on the fold. You should see little droplets of oil land on top of the cocktail. Wipe the peel around the rim to add as much flavour as possible.

BRÛLÉED OR CHARRED FRUIT

One of my favourite garnishes for a serve is a brûléed piece of fruit – sprinkled in sugar and then grilled (broiled) in the oven or charred with a kitchen blowtorch. First, it imparts an incredible aroma to the entire room and will act as a bit of drama for your guests. It also adds a delicious sweet and subtle caramelized flavour to the fruit and the extra texture of a slight crunch. Some great fruits to brûlée for a garnish are small, sweet oranges, clementines and peaches.

Another method is to simply char the fruit with a kitchen torch, which releases the aroma of the fruit and adds a slightly burnt, smoky flavour to your cocktail. A charred pink grapefruit is definitely my favourite, as the char combines perfectly with the fruit's bittersweet characteristics.

GARNISHES

The garnish is such an important aspect of a cocktail, as it is the first thing the drinker sees. Not only is it visually important, but the aroma also introduces you to the cocktail. I am a great believer that a garnish should not just look good but should add flavour to the cocktail, either on its own or by enhancing other flavours.

Apple Fan Garnish: Cut one-quarter from a cored apple. Lay it flat, trim off both ends, then slice lengthways so the remaining slice is 2 cm (¾ in) thick. Cut this into ten 2 mm (⅛ in)-thick slices. Spread out like a fan and stick a cocktail stick through each layer to hold the fan together.

SPARKLING

The origin of the first sparkling cocktail is unclear, but it is most likely the classic Champagne cocktail dating back to 1862. Many variations have been created and enjoyed since then, most famously the French 75, the Kir Royale and the Bellini. It is a genre of cocktail associated with celebrations – and for good reason, with the pop of a cork a familiar sound at many occasions. This chapter takes inspiration from those classic cocktails but, of course, with a non-alcoholic twist.

MARMALADE MIMOSA

SERVES 1 | GLASSWARE: FLUTE GLASS

The mimosa is one of the most iconic brunch cocktails. Although its origins are not completely clear, most credit goes to Frank Meier, a bartender at the Ritz Hotel in Paris, for creating this classic cocktail in 1925. In this non-alcoholic version, both marmalade and freshly squeezed lemon juice have been added to give the serve more complexity and texture – and the result is a delicious, bittersweet and bold flavour of sparkling orange.

INGREDIENTS

1 barspoon orange marmalade
75 ml (2½ fl oz) freshly squeezed
   orange juice
12.5 ml (½ fl oz) freshly squeezed
   lemon juice
75 ml (2½ fl oz) non-alcoholic
   sparkling wine
Orange peel
Orange twist, to garnish

INSTRUCTIONS

Add the orange marmalade, orange juice and lemon juice to a cocktail shaker filled with ice and shake well.

Double strain into a flute glass, pour in the non-alcoholic sparkling wine and stir with a barspoon.

Fold the orange peel in half with the white pith facing outwards and, holding it above the glass, squeeze on the fold to express the oil. You should see little droplets of oil land on top of the cocktail. Garnish with the orange twist.

SUMMER SPRITZ PARTY JUG

SERVES 8 | GLASSWARE: JUG (PITCHER) AND ROCKS (OLD-FASHIONED) GLASSES

The combination of the sweet fruit flavour of the homemade strawberry syrup with the zingy lime juice, refreshing cucumber, bittersweet orange and subtle herbal flavour of mint delivers a beautifully balanced summertime drink. By topping it with non-alcoholic sparkling wine, you'll have the perfect cocktail, whether serving it at a garden party or for an intimate get-together. The ginger ale provides a subtle spice in the background and a long, tasty finish.

INGREDIENTS

½ cucumber, cut into slices
3 strawberries, chopped
½ orange, cut into wedges
1 lime, cut into wedges
10 fresh mint leaves
100 ml (3½ fl oz) Strawberry Syrup (see page 40)
150 ml (5 fl oz) freshly squeezed lime juice
500 ml (17 fl oz) non-alcoholic sparkling wine
250 ml (8½ fl oz) ginger ale
4 strawberries, halved, to garnish

INSTRUCTIONS

Add the cucumber slices, chopped strawberries and orange and lime wedges to the jug.

Clap the mint in your hands and add to the jug. Pour in the strawberry syrup, lime juice, sparkling wine and ginger ale, then top with ice.

Stir well with a barspoon and serve in rocks glasses, each garnished with half a strawberry.

RASPBERRY & THYME BELLINI

SERVES 1 | GLASSWARE: COUPE GLASS

The classic Bellini was invented in 1948 by Giuseppe Cipriani at Harry's Bar in Venice, Italy. Traditionally, it is made with peach, but for this non-alcoholic twist the peach been replaced with a perfect balance of raspberry and thyme. The fresh fruity flavour of raspberry and fermented tea comes from the kombucha, which mixes with the freshly squeezed lime juice to create a delightful drink. The thyme syrup adds sweetness and a subtle herby note in the background.

INGREDIENTS
22.5 ml (¾ fl oz) Thyme Syrup
   (see below)
30 ml (1 fl oz) freshly squeezed
   lime juice
125 ml (4½ fl oz) fizzy raspberry
   kombucha, chilled
Fresh thyme sprig, to garnish

INSTRUCTIONS
Pour the thyme syrup, lime juice and kombucha into a coupe glass and stir with a barspoon. Garnish with a thyme sprig.

THYME SYRUP
MAKES 350 ML (12½ FL OZ)

INGREDIENTS
200 g (1 cup) granulated sugar
240 ml (8 fl oz) water
3 fresh thyme sprigs

INSTRUCTIONS
Add the sugar and water to a saucepan and bring to the boil. Reduce the heat, add the thyme sprigs and simmer, stirring, until the sugar has dissolved. Remove from the heat and leave the thyme to infuse for 30 minutes.

Strain into a clean sterilized glass jar, seal and store in the refrigerator. Use within four weeks.

HUGO'S DRIVING

SERVES 1 | GLASSWARE: WINE GLASS

Along with the Aperol and Limoncello Spritzes, the Hugo has become one of the most popular sparkling cocktails in Italy. This version was inspired by the beautiful classic that originated in the small Alpine town of Naturno in Italy, just south of the Austrian border, which itself was inspired by the elder trees native to the area. The original recipe calls for elderflower cordial (it's since been replaced by liqueur) – so by including it in this recipe, the flavours more closely match the original.

INGREDIENTS
Fresh mint sprig, to muddle
15 ml (½ fl oz) elderflower cordial
  (syrup)
100 ml (3½ fl oz) non-alcoholic
  sparkling wine
30 ml (1 fl oz) soda water (club soda)
Fresh mint sprig, to garnish

INSTRUCTIONS
Add a mint sprig to the wine glass, pour in the elderflower cordial and gently muddle.

Fill the glass with ice cubes and pour in the non-alcoholic sparkling wine, then the soda water. Stir gently with a barspoon. Garnish with the mint sprig.

BLUEBERRY & COCONUT SPRITZ

SERVES 1 | GLASSWARE: ROCKS (OLD-FASHIONED) GLASS

The inspiration for this drink was to create a strong punchy cocktail but one that would be a little different to the usual. The result: a combination of sweet but tart blueberries, freshly squeezed lemon juice and creamy, nutty coconut that makes a complex and deliciously refreshing drink. The bubbles provided by the soda water mixed with the coconut's big, bold flavour creates the perfect match for a great summer cocktail.

INGREDIENTS
1 barspoon blueberry jam
30 ml (1 fl oz) freshly squeezed
  lemon juice
60 ml (2 fl oz) coconut water
Soda water (club soda), to top
3 blueberries, to garnish

FOR THE RIM
Lemon wedge
Desiccated (dry) coconut flakes

INSTRUCTIONS
Coat the rim of the glass by wetting the rim with the lemon wedge and rolling it in coconut flakes.

Add the blueberry jam, lemon juice and coconut water to a shaker filled with ice and shake well.

Add ice cubes to the prepared glass, then double strain the contents of the shaker into the glass and top with soda water.

Stir well with a barspoon and garnish with the blueberries.

CRANBERRY & LAVENDER FIZZ

SERVES 1 | GLASSWARE: FLUTE GLASS

Mixing up the bright, tart flavour of cranberry with the floral and herbal notes of lavender will give you a complex and flavourful cocktail that is ideal for sipping in the spring and summer – in fact, it's a fantastic drink to enjoy in the autumn and winter, too! Lavender has a unique floral note and aroma that complement many different base spirits, plus many people enjoy simply breathing in its scent.

INGREDIENTS

60 ml (2 fl oz) cranberry juice
15 ml (½ fl oz) freshly squeezed
    lime juice
15 ml (½ fl oz) lavender syrup
Soda water (club soda), to top
Lime wheel, to garnish

INSTRUCTIONS

Add the cranberry juice, lime juice and lavender syrup to a cocktail shaker filled with ice and shake. Double strain into the flute glass and top with soda water. Garnish with the lime wheel.

Tip: Lavender is a flavour that can quickly overpower a drink, so take care not to use too much.

CRANBERRY & LAVENDER SYRUP

MAKES 350 ML (12½ FL OZ)

INGREDIENTS

200 g (1 cup) granulated sugar
240 ml (8 fl oz) water
20 g (1½ tbsp) dried lavender

INSTRUCTIONS

Add the sugar, water and dried lavender to a saucepan and bring to the boil. Reduce the heat and simmer, stirring until the sugar has dissolved. Remove from the heat and leave to cool. Strain into a glass jar, seal and store in the refrigerator. Use within four weeks.

LIMON SPRITZ

SERVES 1 | GLASSWARE: WINE GLASS

This fresh sparkling number takes its inspiration from the Limoncello Spritz, the incredibly popular cocktail made with the famous Italian liqueur that is traditionally served as an after-dinner digestivo. In this version, the simple combination of lemon, non-alcoholic sparkling wine and soda is incredibly refreshing and light. The rosemary garnish adds a beautiful herbal fragrance, even before you take your first sip.

INGREDIENTS

30 ml (1 fl oz) freshly squeezed
   lemon juice
22.5 ml (¾ fl oz) Simple Syrup
   (see below)
100 ml (3½ fl oz) non-alcoholic
   sparkling wine
30 ml (1 fl oz) soda water (club soda)
Fresh rosemary sprig, to garnish

INSTRUCTIONS

Fill a wine glass with ice cubes, pour in the fresh lemon juice, simple syrup, non-alcoholic sparkling wine and soda. Stir with a barspoon.

   Clap the rosemary sprig in your hands and use it to garnish.

SIMPLE SYRUP
MAKES 350 ML (12½ FL OZ)

INGREDIENTS

200 g (1 cup) granulated sugar
240 ml (8 fl oz) water

INSTRUCTIONS

Add the sugar and water to a saucepan and bring to the boil. Reduce the heat and simmer, stirring, until the sugar has dissolved. Remove from the heat and leave to cool.

   Decant into a clean sterilized glass jar, seal and store in the refrigerator. Use within four weeks.

GUAVA & PINEAPPLE FIZZ

SERVES 1 | GLASSWARE: COUPE GLASS

This drink is for those who enjoy tropical flavours: the sparkling guava delivers a sweet, flowery taste that is the perfect foil for the classic tiki cocktail flavours of pineapple and freshly squeezed lime juice. It is a cocktail that works all year round, but it's especially good to sip while relaxing under a parasol in the sunshine and imagining yourself on the beach of a tropical island.

INGREDIENTS
15 ml (½ fl oz) grenadine
60 ml (2 fl oz) fresh pineapple juice
15 ml (½ fl oz) freshly squeezed
  lime juice
45 ml (1½ fl oz) sparkling guava
  juice, chilled
Pineapple wedge, to garnish

INSTRUCTIONS
Add the grenadine, pineapple juice and lime juice to a cocktail shaker filled with ice and shake well.

Double strain into a coupe glass, top with the sparkling guava juice and mix well with a barspoon.

Char the pineapple wedge with a kitchen blowtorch and use it to garnish the drink.

MELON & HONEY 75

SERVES 1 | GLASSWARE: FLUTE GLASS

This cocktail has a bold taste that can be compared to the French 75, a classic cocktail named after the 75mm field gun used by the French during the First World War. This non-alcoholic version has the botanical spirit and lemon flavour of the original, but the fresh muddled melon, cloudy apple juice and honey syrup make it a well-rounded serve with big flavour and a long finish.

INGREDIENTS

2 slices honeydew melon, peeled and deseeded
15 ml (½ fl oz) Honey Syrup (see below)
15 ml (½ fl oz) non-alcoholic botanical spirit
30 ml (1 fl oz) cloudy apple juice (apple cider)
22.5 ml (¾ fl oz) freshly squeezed lemon juice
Soda water (club soda), to top
Honeydew melon ball, to garnish

INSTRUCTIONS

Add the melon and honey syrup to a cocktail shaker and muddle. Pour in the botanical spirit, apple juice and lemon juice. Add ice and shake well.
    Double strain into a flute glass and top with soda water. Stir with a barspoon and garnish with the melon ball.

HONEY SYRUP
MAKES 350 ML (12½ FL OZ)

INGREDIENTS

340 g (1 cup) honey
125 ml (4¼ fl oz) water

INSTRUCTIONS

Add the honey and water to a saucepan and bring to the boil. Reduce the heat and simmer, stirring, until dissolved. Remove from the heat and leave to cool. Decant into a clean sterilized glass jar, seal and store in the refrigerator. Use within four weeks.

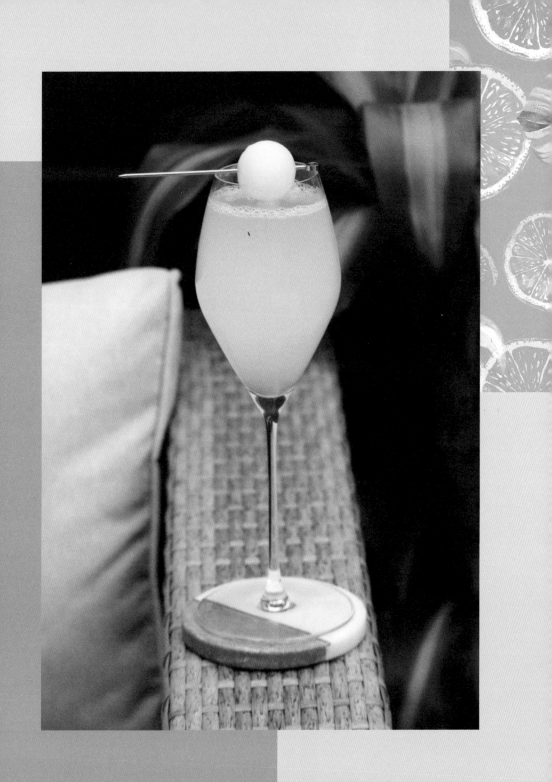

SPARKLING

ROSE WATER & PEACH SPRITZER

SERVES 2 | GLASSWARE: FLUTE GLASSES

Here's a well-rounded balanced cocktail in which the delicate, floral sweetness from the muddled peach is mixed with rose water and freshly squeezed lemon juice, creating what can best be described as a match made in heaven! The rose water has a strong flavour that comes through to give a beautiful long finish, but take care not to use too much as it can over dominate a cocktail – it's all about the balance.

INGREDIENTS
½ fresh peach
30 ml (1 fl oz) Rose Water Syrup (see below)
60 ml (2 fl oz) freshly squeezed lemon juice
Peach sparkling water, to top
Peach wedge, to garnish

INSTRUCTIONS
Cut the peach into cubes, add to a cocktail shaker with the rose water syrup and muddle. Pour in the lemon juice, top with ice and shake well.

Double strain equally into two flute glasses filled with ice and top with peach sparkling water. Mix well with a barspoon and garnish each with a peach wedge.

ROSE WATER SYRUP
MAKES 350 ML (12½ FL OZ)

INGREDIENTS
200 g (1 cup) granulated sugar
120 ml (4 fl oz) rose water
120 ml (4 fl oz) water

INSTRUCTIONS
Add the sugar, rose water and water to a saucepan and bring to the boil. Reduce the heat and simmer, stirring until the sugar has dissolved. Remove from the heat and leave to cool.

Decant into a glass jar, seal and store in the refrigerator. Use within 4 weeks.

38

STRAWBERRY & BASIL TONIC

SERVES 1 | GLASSWARE: HIGHBALL GLASS

The combination of strawberry and basil is a true classic, and for good reason. With the beautiful fruity sweetness from the strawberries and the unique herbal freshness of the basil, it is difficult to think of a better flavour combination. Here is a sparkling cocktail that delivers on both of those big flavours, joined by a little tartness from the lemon, making it a definite crowd-pleaser – even if you're making it only for a crowd of one.

INGREDIENTS

½ lemon
2 strawberries
15 ml (½ fl oz) Simple Syrup
  (see page 32)
8 fresh basil leaves
Mediterranean tonic water, to top
Strawberry, to garnish

INSTRUCTIONS

Cut the lemon in wedges. Add the lemon, strawberries and simple syrup to a highball glass and muddle.

Clap the basil in your hand, add to the glass and top with crushed ice.

Top with Mediterranean tonic water, mix well with a barspoon and garnish with a strawberry.

STRAWBERRY SYRUP

MAKES 300 ML (10 FL OZ)

200 g (1 cup) granulated sugar
240 ml (8 fl oz) water
8 strawberries, cut in half

INSTRUCTIONS

Add the sugar and water to a saucepan and bring to the boil. Reduce the heat to a simmer and stir until the sugar has dissolved. Remove from the heat. Place the strawberries in a clean sealable glass jar, muddle and pour in the sugar syrup mixture. Seal the jar securely and store in the refrigerator for 24 hours.

Strain to remove the strawberries. Decant into a clean sterilized glass jar, seal and store in the refrigerator. Use within three weeks.

BOTANICAL

When thinking of botanicals, you may think of the juniper-flavoured spirit, gin. Luckily, today there are some fantastic non-alcoholic botanical spirits that share gin's many complex ingredients, and they can be used for a twist on some classic cocktails, such as the Tom Collins. This chapter focuses on botanical spirits, with recipes designed to use various fruits and syrups that enhance the herbal flavour and make a well-rounded, tasty cocktail.

RASPBERRY COLLINS

SERVES 1 | GLASSWARE: HIGHBALL GLASS

The first recipe for a Tom Collins was published in 1876, but it dates back to at least 1869 and was supposedly named after a waiter in London. It's simply gin, lemon juice, soda water and sugar syrup, but it really makes the gin the star of the show. This zero-proof twist allows the flavours of the botanical spirit to come through beautifully, and the freshly muddled raspberries take the serve to the next level. It's the perfect drink for enjoying in the spring and summer.

INGREDIENTS
3 raspberries
15 ml (½ fl oz) Simple Syrup
  (see page 32)
60 ml (2 fl oz) non-alcoholic
  botanical spirit
30 ml (1 fl oz) freshly squeezed
  lemon juice
Soda water (club soda), to top
3 raspberries, to garnish

INSTRUCTIONS
Add the raspberries and simple syrup to a cocktail shaker and muddle. Pour in the botanical spirit and lemon juice, top with ice and shake well.

Double strain into a tall glass filled with ice and top with soda water. Garnish with the raspberries.

PEACHES & HONEY PARTY JUG

SERVES 8 | GLASSWARE: JUG (PITCHER) AND STEMMED OR REGULAR WATER GLASSES

Peaches and honey deliver such a delightful combination of flavours to this drink that it's the perfect choice for serving at a party. The deliciously sweet and delicate peach is undoubtedly the star of the cocktail: as peach slices, peach juice and in the fermented peach kombucha, all of which bring a different dynamic. The honey syrup adds a beautiful natural sweetness, and this duo is balanced by the freshly squeezed lemon juice.

INGREDIENTS

300 ml (10 fl oz) non-alcoholic
  botanical spirit
150 ml (5 fl oz) freshly squeezed
  lemon juice
100 ml (3½ fl oz) Honey Syrup
  (see page 36)
300 ml (10 fl oz) peach juice
450 ml (15 fl oz) peach kombucha
2 peaches, stoned and sliced

GARNISH

8 barspoons granulated sugar
8 fresh peach slices

INSTRUCTIONS

Pour the botanical spirit, lemon juice, honey syrup, peach juice and peach kombucha into a jug. Add the sliced peaches with ice cubes, then stir well.

Use a barspoon to coat one side of a peach slice with granulated sugar, then use a kitchen blowtorch to evenly caramelize the sugar.

Serve in water or short stemmed glasses and garnish with the brûléed peach slices.

TANGERINE THYME

SERVES 1 | GLASSWARE: COUPE GLASS

The beautiful flavour of the tangerine is celebrated in this recipe. The honey syrup delivers a subtle herbal background of thyme to the drink and freshly squeezed lemon juice adds the necessary acidity to balance the serve.

INGREDIENTS
4 tangerine wedges
22.5 ml (¾ fl oz) Honey & Thyme Syrup (see below)
50 ml (1¾ fl oz) non-alcoholic botanical spirit
30 ml (1 fl oz) freshly squeezed lemon juice
Tangerine wheel, to garnish

FOR THE RIM
Granulated sugar
Thyme leaves
Lemon wedge

INSTRUCTIONS
Coat the rim of the glass: mix the sugar and thyme leaves together on a saucer or work surface. Wet the rim of the glass with the lemon wedge, then roll in the sugar and thyme leaves.

Add the tangerine wedges and honey and thyme syrup to a cocktail shaker and muddle. Pour in the non-alcoholic botanical spirit and lemon juice, top with ice and shake well.

Double strain into the prepared glass and garnish with a tangerine wheel.

HONEY & THYME SYRUP
MAKES 350 ML (12½ FL OZ)

INGREDIENTS
340 g (1 cup) honey
120 ml (4 fl oz) water
3 fresh thyme sprigs

INSTRUCTIONS
Add the honey and water to a saucepan and bring to the boil. Add the thyme, lower the heat and simmer, stirring, until the sugar has dissolved. Remove from the heat and leave to infuse for 30 minutes. Strain into a clean glass jar, seal and store in the refrigerator. Use within four weeks.

GREEN TEA & MINT LIMEADE

SERVES 1 | GLASSWARE: ROCKS (OLD-FASHIONED) GLASS

Green tea adds a unique, grassy, nutty herbaceousness to cocktails, and you often see it in vodka- and gin-based drinks. The mint combines well with the delicate tea to help bring it to life, and the freshly squeezed lime juice – which is obviously a key component of limeade – adds a lively, citrus element that cuts through all the other ingredients. Green tea can also be infused in a simple syrup to use in your drinks, in the same way as Earl Grey tea (see page 62).

INGREDIENTS

60 ml (2 fl oz) strong-brewed
   green tea
30 ml (1 fl oz) freshly squeezed
   lime juice
22.5 ml (¾ fl oz) Simple Syrup
   (see page 32)
6 fresh mint leaves
Lime tonic water, to top

GARNISH
Lime wheel
Fresh mint sprig

INSTRUCTIONS

Add the green tea, lime juice, simple syrup and mint leaves to a cocktail shaker filled with ice and shake well.

Double strain into a rocks glass filled with ice and top with the lime tonic. Garnish with a lime wheel and mint sprig.

BUTTERFLY PEA FLOWER SOUR

SERVES 1 | GLASSWARE: COUPE GLASS

The butterfly pea flower has become a popular ingredient to add a striking purple colour to spirits and cocktails, and this is definitely the case in this drink, where the butterfly pea syrup creates that epic purple colour. However, the key flavour comes from the non-alcoholic botanical spirit. Adding egg white gives the drink a delicious creamy texture and brings all the flavours together.

INGREDIENTS
60 ml (2 fl oz) non-alcoholic dry
    botanical spirit
22.5 ml (¾ fl oz) Butterfly Pea Syrup
    (see below)
30 ml (1 fl oz) freshly squeezed
    lemon juice
1 egg white or 30 ml (1 fl oz) aquafaba
    (chickpea water)
Edible flowers, such as pansies,
    to garnish

INSTRUCTIONS
Add the botanical spirit, syrup, lemon juice and egg white to a shaker and dry shake (without ice) to whip the egg and combine the ingredients.

   Add ice cubes to the shaker and shake again to chill the cocktail. Double strain into a coupe glass and garnish with an edible flower.

BUTTERFLY PEA SYRUP
MAKES 350 ML (12½ FL OZ)

15 g (1 cup) dried butterfly pea flowers
240 ml (8 fl oz) hot water
200 g (1 cup) granulated sugar

INSTRUCTIONS
Infuse the flowers in the hot water for 5 minutes. Strain, then add to a saucepan with the sugar. Bring to the boil, reduce the heat and simmer for 5 minutes, stirring to dissolve. Remove from the heat and leave to cool. Decant into a clean glass jar, seal and store in the refrigerator. Use within four weeks.

BASIL SMASH

SERVES 1 | GLASSWARE: ROCKS (OLD-FASHIONED) GLASS

This fresh herbal drink is a twist on the delicious Gin Basil Smash, a modern classic invented in 2008 by Jörg Meyer, a bartender in Hamburg, Germany. Basil is the perfect herb to combine with the botanicals found in the spirit, plus it really is the star of this cocktail. It allows the flavour of the botanicals to come through subtly in the background, and mixed with the freshly squeezed lemon juice, this combination will leave you with the most refreshing finish.

INGREDIENTS

8 fresh basil leaves
22.5 ml (¾ fl oz) Simple Syrup
(see page 32)
60 ml (2 fl oz) non-alcoholic
botanical spirit
30 ml (1 fl oz) freshly squeezed
lemon juice
Fresh basil sprig, to garnish

INSTRUCTIONS

Clap the basil in your hands and add to a cocktail shaker with the syrup and gently muddle, without breaking the leaves. Add the botanical spirit, lemon juice and ice, and shake well.

Double strain into a rocks glass filled with crushed ice. Garnish with the basil sprig.

BOTANICAL

RASPBERRY & VANILLA MARTINI

SERVES 1 | GLASSWARE: MARTINI GLASS

This version is a distant cousin of the original Martini, which is thought to have been invented in 1911 at the Knickerbocker Hotel in New York by bartender Martini di Arma di Taggia, who served it to billionaire John D. Rockefeller with equal parts London dry gin and dry vermouth. The botanical flavours are at the forefront of this cocktail, but they are accompanied by sweet, slightly tart raspberries, fresh citrus from the lime juice and a warming sweetness from the vanilla syrup.

INGREDIENTS
3 raspberries
15 ml (½ fl oz) Vanilla Syrup
   (see below)
60 ml (2 fl oz) non-alcoholic
   botanical spirit
30 ml (1 fl oz) freshly squeezed
   lime juice
3 raspberries, to garnish

INSTRUCTIONS
Add the raspberries and vanilla syrup to a shaker and muddle. Pour in the botanical spirit and lime juice, top with ice and shake well.
   Double strain into a Martini glass. Garnish with raspberries.

VANILLA SYRUP
MAKES 350 ML (12½ FL OZ)

INGREDIENTS
200 g (1 cup) granulated sugar
240 ml (8 fl oz) water
1 whole vanilla pod (bean)

INSTRUCTIONS
Add the sugar and water to a saucepan and bring to the boil. Reduce to a simmer, stirring, until the sugar has dissolved. Remove from the heat. Split the vanilla pod in half lengthways, scoop out the seeds and add to the syrup. Leave to infuse for three hours. Strain into a clean glass jar, seal and store in the refrigerator. Use within three weeks.

GARDEN COLLINS

SERVES 1 | GLASSWARE: HIGHBALL GLASS

As the name suggests, this serve is made up of several beautiful flavours that can be found in a typical countryside garden. Along with the natural botanicals in the spirit, there are elderflower, lemon, mint and cucumber to give the cocktail its floral, sweet, herbal and refreshing notes. The combination of ingredients make this the perfect cocktail to enjoy in the sunshine, whether at a garden party or simply relaxing on your own.

INGREDIENTS
2 cucumber slices
15 ml (½ fl oz) elderflower cordial (syrup)
6 fresh mint leaves
60 ml (2 fl oz) non-alcoholic botanical spirit
30 ml (1 fl oz) freshly squeezed lemon juice
Soda water (club soda), to top
Cucumber ribbon (see below), to garnish

INSTRUCTIONS
Add the cucumber slices to a shaker with the elderflower cordial and muddle. Clap the mint in your hands and add to the shaker with the botanical spirit, lemon juice and ice. Shake well.

Double strain into a tall glass filled with ice cubes and top with soda. Garnish with the cucumber ribbon.

CUCUMBER RIBBON

Trim the ends of a whole cucumber. Using a vegetable peeler, slice the cucumber lengthways into one long thin ribbon.

If you are making more than one drink, continue slicing until you reach the seeds, then turn over and repeat on the other side.

You can either thread the ribbon, concertina-style, on a cocktail stick or wrap it around the inside of the glass before you add ice.

MANGO THYME MULE

SERVES 2 | GLASSWARE: ROCKS (OLD-FASHIONED) GLASSES

Here's a different take on the classic Moscow Mule, a 1940s drink that was actually invented in Los Angeles when, as one story goes, John Martin and Jack Morgan brought Smirnoff vodka and ginger beer together at the Cock'n Bull bar to make the new cocktail. This version includes muddled fresh mango, which adds a sweet, tropical flavour, while the thyme adds a herbal undertone that lifts the flavours of both the ginger beer and lime juice.

INGREDIENTS

4 fresh mango slices, each about 2 cm x 1 cm (¾ in x ½ in) thick
30 ml (1 fl oz) Simple Syrup (see page 32)
Fresh thyme sprig
120 ml (4 fl oz) non-alcoholic botanical spirit
60 ml (2 fl oz) freshly squeezed lime juice
Ginger beer, to top
2 fresh thyme sprigs, to garnish

INSTRUCTIONS

Add the mango and simple syrup to a shaker and muddle. Clap the thyme sprig in your hands and add to the shaker, then pour in the botanical spirit and lime juice. Top with ice and shake well.

Double strain into rocks glasses filled with ice cubes. Top with ginger beer, mix well with a barspoon and garnish with a thyme sprig.

EARL OF BRAMBLE

SERVES 1 | GLASSWARE: ROCKS GLASS

This serve was inspired by the classic Bramble, which was created by Dick Bradsell in 1984 at the bar of Fred's Club in Soho, London. Dick's inspiration came from his memories of picking blackberries on the Isle of Wight as a child. For this non-alcoholic twist, the simple syrup has been replaced by an Earl Grey tea syrup, which adds a wonderful black tea and citrussy bergamot flavour. The sweetness of the muddled blackberries balances well with the tart lemon juice.

INGREDIENTS
3 blackberries
22.5 ml (¾ fl oz) Earl Grey Tea Syrup (see below)
60 ml (2 fl oz) non-alcoholic botanical spirit
30 ml (1 fl oz) freshly squeezed lemon juice

GARNISH
3 blackberries
Fresh mint sprig

INSTRUCTIONS
Add the blackberries and Earl Grey syrup to a rocks glass and muddle. Top with crushed ice and pour in the botanical spirit and lemon juice, then mix well with a barspoon.

Add a straw, top with crushed ice and garnish with blackberries and a mint sprig.

EARL GREY TEA SYRUP
MAKES 350 ML (12½ FL OZ)

INGREDIENTS
240 ml (8 fl oz) strong-brewed Earl Grey tea
200 g (1 cup) granulated sugar

INSTRUCTIONS
Add the strong Earl Grey tea and sugar to a saucepan and bring to the boil. Simmer, stirring, until the sugar has dissolved, then remove from heat. Decant into a clean sterilized glass jar, seal and store in the refrigerator. Use within three weeks.

TROPICAL

When thinking of tropical cocktails, many of us think of sipping our drinks at a beach bar in some exotic, beach-side destination, with perhaps a mini umbrella in our glass. Although there are no mini umbrellas in sight here, this chapter should still help you get in the tropical spirit, taking classic rum cocktails and twisting them to include all those tropical flavours without the alcohol. This chapter includes many recipes – with flavours such as pineapple, coconut and mango – that are perfect to enjoy with friends, especially in those summer months.

PINEAPPLE & GINGER MOJITO

SERVES 8 | GLASSWARE: JUG (PITCHER) AND ROCKS (OLD-FASHIONED) GLASSES

The origin of the Mojito isn't 100 per cent clear, but one theory claims it can be traced back to 16th-century Cuba and the cocktail named El Draque. This non-alcoholic twist on the classic is the perfect cocktail for a party, offering the big tropical flavour of the pineapple, freshness from the lime, a kick of herbs from the fresh mint and a warmth that comes through from the ginger beer.

INGREDIENTS

2 limes, cut into 10 wheels
¼ pineapple, cut into 10 wedges
20 fresh mint leaves
500 ml (17 fl oz) pineapple juice
150 ml (5 fl oz) freshly squeezed
   lime juice
100 ml (3½ fl oz) Simple Syrup
   (see page 32)
250 ml (8½ fl oz) ginger beer

GARNISH

8 pineapple wedges
8 mint leaves

INSTRUCTIONS

Add the lime wheels and pineapple wedges to a jug. Clap the mint in your hands and add to the jug, then pour in the pineapple juice, lime juice and simple syrup.

Add ice and top with ginger beer. Stir well with a barspoon.

Serve each glass garnished with a pineapple wedge and mint sprig.

BLUE HAWAIIAN

SERVES 1 | GLASSWARE: HIGHBALL GLASS

Want an impressive cocktail with the tropical flavours of coconut and pineapple that are found in a Piña Colada? Look no further than the Blue Hawaiian, where coconut and pineapple are combined beautifully with the orange flavour of blue Curaçao, making it the perfect tiki combination. The non-alcoholic Curaçao syrup gives the serve not only a subtle orange flavour but a fantastic bright blue colour – which is why this vibrant cocktail can easily be described as a real showstopper.

INGREDIENTS

30 ml (1 fl oz) non-alcoholic white cane spirit

15 ml (½ fl oz) non-alcoholic blue Curaçao syrup

15 ml (½ fl oz) freshly squeezed lime juice

45 ml (1½ fl oz) pineapple juice

30 ml (1 fl oz) cream of coconut

GARNISH

Pineapple wedge
Pineapple leaf
Maraschino cherry

INSTRUCTIONS

Add the white cane spirit, blue Curaçao syrup, lime juice, pineapple juice and cream of coconut to a cocktail shaker filled with ice and shake well to chill.

Double strain into a tall glass filled with crushed ice. Garnish with a pineapple wedge, pineapple leaf and maraschino cherry.

PASSION FRUIT MOJITO

SERVES 1 | GLASSWARE: HIGHBALL GLASS

The tropical citrus flavour of passion fruit makes it a fantastic choice for cocktails, and it works especially well in this Mojito. Here the fruit's flavour works magic with the flavour coming from the white cane spirit, and adding the freshly squeezed lime juice and the simple syrup creates a well-balanced serve. The mint provides a subtle herbal background to the cocktail, and as a garnish it gives off a beautiful aroma, tempting you to take your first sip!

INGREDIENTS

1 lime, cut into cubes
Seeds and pulp of ½ passion fruit
15 ml (½ fl oz) Simple Syrup
   (see page 32)
6 fresh mint leaves
60 ml (2 fl oz) non-alcoholic white
   cane spirit
30 ml (1 fl oz) soda water (club soda)

GARNISH

½ passion fruit
Fresh mint sprig

INSTRUCTIONS

Add the lime cubes to a tall glass with the seeds and pulp from the half passion fruit. Add the simple syrup, then muddle.

Clap the mint in your hands, add to the glass and fill the glass three-quarters full with crushed ice. Pour in the white cane spirit and soda, then stir well with a barspoon to combine the ingredients.

Top with more crushed ice, garnish with the half passion fruit and a mint sprig and serve with a straw.

KIWI DAIQUIRI

SERVES 1 | GLASSWARE: COUPE GLASS

Here's a cocktail based on the classic Daiquiri, which was named after the location it was created, the town of Daiquiri on the south-eastern tip of Cuba – where it was supposedly invented in 1898 by an American mining engineer named Jennings Cox. In this version of the classic, it is all about the tropical flavour of the kiwi fruit, which combines perfectly with the non-alcoholic white cane spirit and lime. The honey is subtle but gives the serve a natural sweetness.

INGREDIENTS
½ kiwi fruit, peeled and chopped
22.5 ml (¾ fl oz) Honey Syrup
    (see page 36)
60 ml (2 fl oz) non-alcoholic white
    cane spirit
30 ml (1 fl oz) freshly squeezed
    lime juice
Kiwi slice, to garnish

INSTRUCTIONS
Add the kiwi and honey syrup to a cocktail shaker and muddle. Pour in the white cane spirit and lime juice, top with ice and shake well.
    Double strain into a coupe glass and garnish with the kiwi slice.

FROZEN PIÑA COLADA

SERVES 2 | GLASSWARE: BALLOON OR ROCKS (OLD-FASHIONED) GLASSES

Like the original Piña Colada, this twist on the famous cocktail combines pineapple and coconut. There are several claims for its invention, but the most believable one is from the Caribe Hilton in San Juan, Puerto Rico, where in 1954 Ramon Marrero created a drink for the guests on holiday there. As it was originally made for the whole family to enjoy – the rum was added afterwards – this non-alcoholic recipe is closer to the first Piña Colada than the recipe everybody follows today.

INGREDIENTS
90 ml (3 fl oz) coconut cream
120 ml (4 fl oz) pineapple juice
6 frozen pineapple chunks
30 ml (1 fl oz) freshly squeezed
　　lime juice
30 ml (1 fl oz) Simple Syrup
　　(see page 32)

GARNISH
2 pineapple wedges
2 cherries

INSTRUCTIONS
Add the coconut cream, pineapple juice, frozen pineapple, lime juice, simple syrup and a handful of ice to a blender and blend until smooth.

Pour into two rocks glasses. Add straws and garnish each with a pineapple wedge and a cherry.

LYCHEE MOJITO

SERVES 1 | GLASSWARE: HIGHBALL GLASS

With its unique, sweet and musky flavour, the lychee is a fruit that tastes like a cross between strawberry and pear with rose water mixed in – which makes it the perfectly balanced fruit for a Mojito. It also goes well with the hints of caramel from the demerara sugar syrup. The lime and soda water add a refreshing characteristic, and the mint leaves give the cocktail a herbal long finish.

INGREDIENTS
½ lime, cut into cubes
2 fresh lychees, peeled and chopped
15 ml (½ fl oz) Demerara Sugar Syrup
(see below)
6 fresh mint leaves
50 ml (1¾ fl oz) lychee juice
Soda water (club soda), to top

GARNISH
Whole lychee, peeled
Fresh mint sprig

INSTRUCTIONS
Add the lime cubes to a tall glass with the lychees and the demerara sugar syrup, then muddle.

Clap the mint in your hands, add to the glass and top with crushed ice. Pour in the lychee juice and soda and stir well with a barspoon to combine the ingredients.

Add a straw, top with crushed ice and garnish with a lychee and a mint sprig.

DEMERARA SUGAR SYRUP

MAKES 250 ML (12½ FL OZ)

INGREDIENTS
200 g (1 cup) demerara sugar
240 ml (8 fl oz) water

INSTRUCTIONS
Add the sugar and water to a saucepan and bring to the boil. Reduce the heat and simmer, stirring, for 5 minutes until the sugar has dissolved. Remove from the heat and leave to cool. Decant into a clean sterilized glass jar, seal and store in the refrigerator. Use within four weeks.

FROZEN MANGO DAIQUIRI

SERVES 1 | GLASSWARE: COUPE GLASS

Looking for a drink that is perfect for relaxing with in the sunshine? Here is a tropical twist on the original Daiquiri, where frozen mango becomes the true champion of the cocktail. The fruit is undeniably enhanced by the flavours that come through from the white cane spirit and refreshing lime juice. By blending the ingredients of this cocktail, you'll get a drink with a silky texture that adds the perfect finishing touch.

INGREDIENTS
60 ml (2 fl oz) non-alcoholic white
    cane spirit
4 frozen mango chunks
30 ml (1 fl oz) freshly squeezed
    lime juice
22.5 ml (¾ fl oz) Simple Syrup
    (see page 32)
Lime wheel, to garnish

INSTRUCTIONS
Add the white cane spirit, mango, lime juice, simple syrup and a handful of cubed ice to a blender and blend for 45 seconds or until it is a smooth, even consistency.
    Pour into a coupe glass and garnish with a lime wheel.

COCONUT & WATERMELON MARTINI

SERVES 1 | GLASSWARE: MARTINI GLASS

Tropical flavours often work well together, and this is true when combining watermelon with coconut in this drink. The nutty coconut flavour is at the forefront, but the watermelon really stands up against it. The watermelon syrup offers not just sweetness but also depth of flavour, because no water is added – just the liquid from the fruit. There is also a subtle warming spice in the background from the vanilla in the syrup.

INGREDIENTS

2 watermelon wedges
15 ml (½ fl oz) Watermelon & Vanilla Syrup (see below)
60 ml (2 fl oz) coconut water
15 ml (½ fl oz) cream of coconut
22.5 ml (¾ fl oz) freshly squeezed lime juice
Watermelon wedge, to garnish

INSTRUCTIONS

Add the watermelon wedges to a cocktail shaker with the watermelon and vanilla syrup and muddle. Pour in the coconut water, cream of coconut and lime juice. Top with ice and shake well.

Double strain into a Martini glass and garnish with a watermelon wedge.

WATERMELON & VANILLA SYRUP

MAKES 300 ML (10½ FL OZ)

INGREDIENTS

1 vanilla pod (bean)
300 g (2 cups) watermelon cubes
400 g (2 cups) granulated sugar

INSTRUCTIONS

Split the vanilla pod lengthways and scrape out the seeds into a bowl. Add the watermelon and sugar, stirring well to evenly coat the watermelon. Cover and leave for 2 hours.

Strain to remove the watermelon pieces. Pour into a clean sterilized glass bottle, seal and store in the refrigerator. Use within two weeks.

CLEMENTINE & MARMALADE MOJITO

SERVES 1 | GLASSWARE: HIGHBALL GLASS

Looking for a drink that has all the characteristics of a Mojito but with a bittersweet flavour? Look no further: the lime and mint add a refreshing, herbal flavour similar to the original, but by using orange marmalade, freshly squeezed clementine juice and clementine tonic, the serve has an intense, layered orange flavour. Charring the clementine for the garnish creates such an incredible aroma that you'll want to start drinking this Mojito as soon as it is made.

INGREDIENTS

½ lime, cut into cubes
1 barspoon marmalade
6 fresh mint leaves
60 ml (2 fl oz) freshly squeezed
   clementine juice
7.5 ml (¼ fl oz) Simple Syrup
   (see page 32)
Clementine tonic, to top
Clementine wheel, to garnish

INSTRUCTIONS

Add the lime cubes to a tall glass with the marmalade and muddle. Clap the mint in your hands, add to the glass and top with crushed ice. Pour in the clementine juice and simple syrup and stir with a barspoon to combine all the ingredients. Add a straw and top with clementine tonic and crushed ice.

Char the clementine wheel with a kitchen blowtorch and use it to garnish the cocktail.

AGAVE

A natural sweetener, agave comes in both light and dark varieties. Light agave has a mild sweetness, whereas dark agave has a stronger, caramel-like flavour. When agave and cocktails are mentioned together, many of us instantly think of well-known classics such as a Margarita, or perhaps a Paloma. Thankfully, it is possible to create non-alcoholic versions with the same strong, recognizable flavours, using some beautiful non-alcoholic agave spirits.

SPICED HIBISCUS MARGARITA

SERVES 1 | GLASSWARE: ROCKS (OLD-FASHIONED) GLASS

This serve is inspired by the classic Margarita, invented by Francisco 'Pancho' Morales on 4 July 1942 at Tommy's Place, a bar in Juárez, Mexico. For this version, the tropical hibiscus adds a sweet and slightly tart flavour, and the cinnamon syrup a subtle warming spice.

INGREDIENTS
45 ml (1 ½ fl oz) non-alcoholic
    agave spirit
30 ml (1 fl oz) freshly squeezed
    lime juice
45 ml (1½ fl oz) strong hibiscus tea
22.5 ml (¾ fl oz) Cinnamon Syrup
    (see below)
Hibiscus flower (in syrup), to garnish

FOR THE RIM
Lime wedge
Sea salt

INSTRUCTIONS
Coat the rim of the glass: wet half the rim with lime and roll it in the salt.

Add the agave spirit, lime juice, hibiscus tea and cinnamon syrup to a cocktail shaker filled with ice cubes and shake.

Add ice cubes to the prepared rocks glass and double strain the cocktail ingredients into the glass. Garnish with a hibiscus flower.

CINNAMON SYRUP
MAKES 350 ML (12½ FL OZ)

INGREDIENTS
200 g (1 cup) granulated sugar
240 ml (1 cup) water
4 cinnamon sticks

INSTRUCTIONS
Bring the sugar and water to a boil in a saucepan. Add the cinnamon sticks and simmer for 5 minutes, stirring until the sugar has dissolved. Remove and leave to infuse for 3 hours. Strain into a clean sterilized glass bottle, seal and store in the refrigerator. Use within four weeks.

MANGO & CHILLI SMASH

SERVES 1 | GLASSWARE: ROCKS (OLD-FASHIONED) GLASS

Agave and chilli form a flavour combination that is a match made in heaven. For this cocktail, the red chilli adds a spicy background heat but without overpowering the key ingredient: the mango. This delicious tropical fruit has a succulent, sweet aromatic flavour that is a real crowd-pleaser, and by combining it with the agave spirit, agave syrup and lime juice, you'll have a beautifully balanced serve that packs a lot of flavour.

INGREDIENTS

2 fresh mango slices, measuring about 2 cm x 1 cm (¾ in x ½ in)
2 fresh red chilli slices
22.5 ml (¾ fl oz) agave syrup
60 ml (2 fl oz) non-alcoholic agave spirit
30 ml (1 fl oz) freshly squeezed lime juice
Tonic water, to top
Whole red chilli, to garnish

INSTRUCTIONS

Add the mango, chilli slices and agave syrup to a cocktail shaker and muddle. Add the agave spirit, lime juice and ice cubes and shake.

Double strain into a rocks glass filled with ice cubes, top with tonic water and stir with a barspoon. Garnish with a red chilli.

PALOMA PITCHER

**SERVES 8 | GLASSWARE: JUG (PITCHER) AND
ROCKS (OLD-FASHIONED) GLASS**

Although the Paloma's origin is unknown, some believe it's named after
'La Paloma' (The Dove), a popular Spanish folk song composed in the early
1860s. Others believe it was created in the 1950s by the legendary Don Javier
Delgado Corona, owner of La Capilla in Tequila, Mexico. Either way, this
beautiful, bittersweet serve is one of the most popular tequila cocktails in the
world. This non-alcoholic twist has the same burst of flavour as the classic, with
the pink grapefruit and agave being the stars of the show.

INGREDIENTS
1 pink grapefruit, cut into slices
1 lime, cut into wheels
300 ml (10 fl oz) non-alcoholic
  agave spirit
225 ml (7 ½ fl oz) pink grapefruit juice
150 ml (5 fl oz) freshly squeezed
  lime juice
100 ml (3½ fl oz) agave syrup
300 ml (10 fl oz) grapefruit soda
  water (club soda)
8 lime wheels, to garnish

FOR THE RIM
Lime wedge
Pink Himalayan salt

INSTRUCTIONS
Coat the rim of each glass: wet half
the rim using the lime wedge and roll
it in the pink Himalayan salt.

  Add the pink grapefruit slices
and lime wheels to a jug. Fill the jug
with ice cubes and pour in the agave
spirit, pink grapefruit juice, lime
juice, agave syrup and grapefruit
soda. Stir well with a barspoon to
combine the ingredients.

  Serve the cocktails in the prepared
glasses, garnished with lime wheels.

STRAWBERRY & HONEY MARGARITA

SERVES 1 | GLASSWARE: COUPE GLASS

For this fruity twist on a classic Margarita, the freshly muddled, sweet strawberry flavour comes through as the main taste. Replacing the agave with honey syrup gives a different dynamic, with a bigger natural sweet flavour coming through, which is perfectly balanced with the fresh lime juice. Like all true Margaritas, the rim of the glass is salted, which was originally to counterbalance any bitterness in the original recipe's ingredients. It's your choice which side of the rim to drink from.

INGREDIENTS

3 strawberries, leaves removed
22.5 ml (¾ fl oz) Honey Syrup
  (see page 36)
60 ml (2 fl oz) non-alcoholic
  agave spirit
30 ml (1 fl oz) freshly squeezed
  lime juice
½ strawberry, to garnish

FOR THE RIM
Lime wedge
Sea salt

INSTRUCTIONS

Coat the rim of the glass: wet half the rim with lime wedge and roll in the sea salt.

Add the strawberries and honey syrup to a cocktail shaker and muddle. Pour in the agave spirit and lime juice, top with ice cubes and shake well.

Double strain into the prepared glass and garnish with the strawberry.

AGAVE

FROZEN MAPLEBERRY

SERVES 1 | GLASSWARE: COUPE GLASS

Combining raspberries and maple syrup may make this cocktail seem almost like a dessert – however, add agave spirit and the flavour comes through beautifully. The raspberry tea brings a sweet, tangy, slightly tart aspect that is lifted by the freshly squeezed lemon juice. This is the perfect frozen cocktail to enjoy in the sunshine, and the mint sprig garnish adds a fresh herbal aroma.

INGREDIENTS
45 ml (1½ fl oz) non-alcoholic
  agave spirit
4 frozen raspberries
30 ml (1 fl oz) frozen lemon juice
45 ml (1½ fl oz) strong-brewed
  raspberry tea
22.5 ml (¾ fl oz) maple syrup

GARNISH
2 fresh raspberries
Fresh mint sprig

INSTRUCTIONS
Add the agave spirit, frozen raspberries, lemon juice, raspberry tea, maple syrup and 2 cups of cubed ice to a blender and blend for 45 seconds or until it has reached a smooth, even consistency.

Pour into a coupe glass and garnish with the raspberries and a mint sprig.

PINEAPPLE MARGARITA

SERVES 2 | GLASSWARE: ROCKS (OLD-FASHIONED) GLASSES

This non-alcoholic twist on the original Margarita combines the marvellous flavour of agave with the sweet and acidic tropical pineapple. So often used in tiki rum-based cocktails, the pineapple also works well in a Margarita. Its strong flavour is at the forefront of the drink and balances well with the lime juice and agave syrup, while the salted rim helps to cut through the acid and sweetness.

INGREDIENTS
120 ml (4 fl oz) non-alcoholic agave
   spirit
90 ml (3 fl oz) pineapple juice
30 ml (1 fl oz) freshly squeezed
   lime juice
22.5 ml (¾ fl oz) agave syrup
2 pineapple wedges, to garnish

FOR THE RIM
Lime wedge
Himalayan salt

INSTRUCTIONS
Coat the rim of each glass: wet half the rim using the lime wedge and roll in the Himalayan salt.

Pour the agave spirit, pineapple juice, lime juice and agave syrup into a cocktail shaker filled with ice cubes and shake well.

Add ice cubes to the prepared rocks glasses and double strain the cocktail equally between them. Garnish each with a pineapple wedge.

PASSION FRUIT PALOMA

SERVES 1 | GLASSWARE: HIGHBALL GLASS

The introduction of tropical passion fruit adds another dynamic to the classic Paloma. The fruit has an intense, aromatic and tart flavour that becomes the key note in any cocktail. Combining it with the bitter grapefruit, citrussy lime juice and sweet agave syrup creates a complex and well-balanced serve, and with the simple half passion fruit garnish and striking colour, it is certainly a showstopper of a drink.

INGREDIENTS

Seeds and pulp of ½ passion fruit
60 ml (2 fl oz) freshly squeezed pink grapefruit juice
15 ml (½ fl oz) freshly squeezed lime juice
15 ml (½ fl oz) agave syrup
Soda water (club soda), to top
½ passion fruit, to garnish

INSTRUCTIONS

Add the passion fruit seeds and pulp to a cocktail shaker, then pour in the pink grapefruit juice, lime juice and agave syrup. Top with ice cubes and shake well.

Double strain into a tall glass filled with ice cubes and top with soda water. Stir with a barspoon to combine the ingredients. Garnish with half a passion fruit.

WATERMELON & CHILLI MARGARITA

SERVES 1 | GLASSWARE: COUPE GLASS

Watermelon and agave spirit are an interesting pairing: the watermelon allows
the agave to stand up as the main ingredient and flavour of the cocktail, plus it
adds a refreshing sweetness in the background. The red chilli provides a lovely
subtle heat, and by coating only half the rim with the chilli-salt mix, you have
the choice to add a little more spice or not. Take a bite of the watermelon
garnish to cleanse your palate so you can enjoy the big flavours more intensely
on your next sip.

INGREDIENTS
2 watermelon slices
2 fresh red chilli slices
22.5 ml (¾ fl oz) Simple Syrup
   (see page 32)
60 ml (2 fl oz) non-alcoholic
   agave spirit
30 ml (1 fl oz) freshly squeezed
   lime juice
Watermelon wedge, to garnish

FOR THE RIM
Chilli salt
Watermelon juice

INSTRUCTIONS
Coat the rim of the glass: tip some
chilli salt onto a small plate or work
surface. Wet half the rim with
watermelon juice and roll it in the
chilli-salt mix.

Add the watermelon slices, red chilli
slices and simple syrup to a cocktail
shaker and muddle. Pour in the agave
spirit and lime juice. Top with ice and
shake well.

Double strain into the prepared
glass and garnish with a watermelon
wedge.

Tip: If you can't find ready-made
chilli salt, combine sea salt with finely
crushed chilli flakes. Alternatively use
Tajín seasoning, a delicious spicy mix
of dried chillies, lime and sea salt.

BITTERSWEET

Bittersweet cocktails have been thought of as an acquired taste in the past, but this genre of cocktails seems to now be the one with the most growth, with classics such as the Negroni and the Aperol Spritz helping them gain in popularity. This chapter celebrates the bittersweet flavour – think grapefruit, blood orange, marmalade, aromatic bitters and all things sugary-sharp, paired with some delicious non-alcohol spirits.

JUNGLE BIRD

SERVES 1 | GLASSWARE: ROCKS (OLD-FASHIONED) GLASS

This serve is inspired by the Jungle Bird, created in 1973 by Jeffrey Ong at the Kuala Lumpur Hilton and served in the Aviary Bar. The cocktail was reportedly served inside a bird-shaped porcelain vessel, hence the drink's name. For this non-alcoholic version, the bitter aperitif and pineapple create the tropical, bittersweet flavour, and the spiced pineapple syrup adds the warming spices you would get from the rum in the classic version.

INGREDIENTS
45 ml (1 ½ fl oz) non-alcoholic bitter aperitif

45 ml (1 ½ fl oz) pineapple juice

22.5ml (¾ fl oz) freshly squeezed lime juice

22.5ml (¾ fl oz) Spiced Pineapple Syrup (see below)

TO GARNISH
1 wedge fresh pineapple

1 barspoon granulated sugar

INSTRUCTIONS
Add the bitter aperitif, pineapple juice, lime juice and spiced pineapple syrup to a cocktail shaker filled with ice cubes and shake well.

Double strain into a rocks glass filled with ice cubes.

Roll the pineapple in the granulated sugar to coat evenly. Use a kitchen blowtorch to carefully caramelize the slice on both sides. Garnish and serve.

SPICED PINEAPPLE SYRUP
MAKES 300 ML (10½ FL OZ)

INGREDIENTS
1 whole ripe pineapple, peeled, core removed and sliced into chunks

Zest of 1 lime

¾ cup (150 g) demerara sugar

INSTRUCTIONS
Add the pineapple, lime zest and sugar to a glass bowl and stir to combine. Cover with clingfilm (plastic wrap) and leave at room temperature for 12 hours. Strain into a clean sterilized glass bottle, seal and store in the refrigerator. Use within two weeks.

APRICOT GARIBALDI

SERVES 1 | GLASSWARE: HIGHBALL GLASS

Here is a non-alcoholic version of the classic Garibaldi, the two-ingredient Italian cocktail made with Campari and orange juice. The original serve was named after Giuseppe Garibaldi, a general who contributed to the unification of Italy back in 1871. For this twist on the classic, the non-alcoholic bitter aperitif replaces the Campari, and the introduction of the apricot jam adds a delightful texture and depth of flavour. It works especially well as a brunch cocktail.

INGREDIENTS
1 barspoon apricot jam
90 ml (3 fl oz) freshly squeezed
    orange juice
45 ml (1½ fl oz) non-alcoholic
    bitter apertif
Orange wedge, to garnish

INSTRUCTIONS
Add a barspoon of apricot jam and the orange juice to a cocktail shaker with one ice cube and shake well to combine and aerate.

Pour the bitter aperitif into a tall glass filled with ice cubes and top with the contents of the shaker. Garnish with an orange wedge.

GRAPEFRUIT & ROSEMARY SOUR

SERVES 1 | GLASSWARE: COUPE GLASS

The pairing of pink grapefruit with rosemary is one that has become extremely popular in cocktails, and for good reason. For this non-alcoholic serve, the botanicals in the spirit are at the forefront, balanced by the bittersweetness of the grapefruit and the sweet and herbaceous rosemary syrup. It's all bought together with the silky texture from the egg white, and the charred grapefruit garnish gives the drink an enticing aroma.

INGREDIENTS

60 ml (2 fl oz) non-alcoholic botanical spirit
45 ml (1½ fl oz) freshly squeezed pink grapefruit juice
15 ml (½ fl oz) freshly squeezed lemon juice
22.5 ml (¾ fl oz) Rosemary Syrup (see below)
1 egg white or 30 ml (1 fl oz) aquafaba (chickpea water)
Grapefruit wedge, to garnish

INSTRUCTIONS

Add the botanical spirit, pink grapefruit juice, lemon juice, rosemary syrup and egg white to a cocktail shaker and dry shake.

Add ice cubes and shake again to chill the cocktail.

Double strain into a coupe glass.

Char the grapefruit wedge with a kitchen blowtorch and use as a garnish.

ROSEMARY SYRUP

MAKES 350 ML (12½ FL OZ)

INGREDIENTS

200 g (1 cup) granulated sugar
240 ml (8 fl oz) water
3 rosemary sprigs

INSTRUCTIONS

Add the sugar, water and rosemary to a saucepan and bring to the boil. Reduce to a simmer and stir until the sugar has dissolved. Remove from the heat and leave for 30 minutes. Strain into a clean glass bottle, seal and store in the refrigerator. Use within four weeks.

NOGRONI

SERVES 2 | GLASSWARE: ROCKS (OLD-FASHIONED) GLASSES

The inspiration for this cocktail is the infamous Negroni, which was reportedly invented in the early 20th century by Count Camillo Negroni. While at Bar Casoni in Florence, he demanded that the bartender strengthen his favourite cocktail, the Americano, by replacing the soda water with gin. For this mocktail twist, the non-alcoholic botanical spirit, Italian orange apertivio and aperitif offer all the flavours found in the classic, but without the alcohol. The expressed orange oil adds an intense bittersweet orange aroma.

INGREDIENTS
60 ml (2 fl oz) non-alcoholic botanical spirit
60 ml (2 fl oz) non-alcoholic Italian orange aperitivo
60 ml (2 fl oz) non-alcoholic Apéritif Rosso
Orange peel
2 orange twists, to garnish

INSTRUCTIONS
Add the botanical spirit, Italian orange aperitivo and Apéritif Rosso to a mixing glass, fill with ice cubes and stir for 45 seconds.

Pour equally into two rocks glasses filled with ice cubes.

To express the orange oil from the orange peel, fold the peel in half with the white pith facing outwards and, holding it above the glass, squeeze on the fold to express the oil. You should see little droplets of oil released in a puffy cloud. Garnish the drinks with the orange twists.

Tip: If the cocktail ingredients are all clear, stirring them in a mixing glass will chill the cocktail but retain their clarity, whereas shaking will turn them cloudy.

BLOOD ORANGE FIZZ

SERVES 1 | GLASSWARE: ROCKS (OLD-FASHIONED) GLASS

Blood orange has a complex flavour that tastes like both orange and pink grapefruit, making it a great ingredient for a bittersweet cocktail. Here, it is combined with tart lime juice and balanced with sweet syrup. The egg white gives the drink a silky texture and also creates foam on top. When the soda water is poured in, the foam rises above the rim, creating a beautiful finish. It is also strong enough to hold a garnish, making a showstopper of a cocktail.

INGREDIENTS

60 ml (2 fl oz) freshly squeezed
   blood orange juice
30 ml (1 fl oz) freshly squeezed
   lime juice
22.5 ml (¾ fl oz) Simple Syrup
   (see page 32)
1 egg white or 30 ml (1 fl oz) aquafaba
   (chickpea water)
Indian tonic water, to top
Dehydrated blood orange wheel,
   to garnish

INSTRUCTIONS

Add the blood orange juice, lime juice, simple syrup and egg white to a cocktail shaker and dry shake (without ice).

Add ice cubes, shake again to chill and pour into a rocks glass.

Let the cocktail settle for 45 seconds, then pour in the tonic water slowly until the foam has risen above the rim.

Thread a straw through the centre of the dehydrated blood orange wheel and carefully add to the cocktail.

CLEMENTINE SPRITZ PARTY JUG

SERVES 8 | GLASSWARE: JUG (PITCHER) AND WINE GLASSES

The Spritz originated in Italy in the 19th century as a way to water down sparkling wine. Today the Aperol Spritz – with its bittersweet flavour infused with sparkling wine and soda water – has become one of the most popular cocktails in the world. This non-alcoholic spritz mixes the bittersweet flavour of the aperitif with clementine juice, which allows the deliciously sweet clementine flavour to be the star of the show. The rosemary sprig garnish adds a herbal aroma, giving the drink freshness.

INGREDIENTS

225 ml (7½ fl oz) clementine juice
300 ml (10 fl oz) non-alcoholic bittersweet aperitif
450 ml (15 fl oz) non-alcoholic sparking wine
150 ml (5 fl oz) soda water (club soda)
2 clementines, sliced
8 rosemary sprigs, to garnish

INSTRUCTIONS

Pour the clementine juice, bittersweet aperitif, sparkling wine and soda water into a jug. Add the clementine slices and ice cubes and stir well with a barspoon.

Serve in wine glasses, garnished with rosemary sprigs.

DARK & SPICY

This chapter pays homage to the darker spirits, such as whisky, which work perfectly in classics such as the Old Fashioned and the Manhattan. These work very well with different spices and with the introduction of non-alcoholic spirits such as malt spirit, so it has never been a better time to mix up a zero-proof cocktail. This section has many different spiced syrup recipes, as they are a great addition to help create a balanced but intense, flavoursome non-alcoholic cocktail.

NEW YORK SOUR

SERVES 1 | GLASSWARE: ROCKS (OLD-FASHIONED) GLASS

This non-alcoholic serve is inspired by the classic New York Sour, which is a late 19th-century update of the Whisky Sour, with red wine added as a float. The wine lends its aromatic qualities and deep red colour to the drink. Unlike other layered cocktails that are usually stirred into the drink, the New York Sour is designed to be drunk through the red wine. This twist has the malty, citrussy flavour of the original, and the non-alcoholic red wine creates the same striking float.

INGREDIENTS

60 ml (2 fl oz) non-alcoholic
    malt spirit
30 ml (1 fl oz) freshly squeezed
    lemon juice
15 ml (½ fl oz) Spiced Simple Syrup
    (see below)
Non-alcoholic red wine, for the float

INSTRUCTIONS

Add the malt spirit, lemon juice and spiced simple syrup to a shaker filled with ice and shake well. Double strain into a rocks glass filled with ice.

Layer the non-alcoholic red wine over the top of the cocktail, pouring it over the back of a barspoon so it floats on top of the drink.

SPICED SIMPLE SYRUP
MAKES 350 ML (12½ FL OZ)

INGREDIENTS

200 g (1 cup) granulated sugar
240 ml (8 fl oz) water
1 cinnamon stick
2 cloves
1 star anise
3 orange peel strips

INSTRUCTIONS

Add all the syrup ingredients to a saucepan and bring to the boil. Reduce to a simmer and stir for 5 minutes, until the sugar has dissolved. Remove from the heat and leave to infuse for 30 minutes. Strain into a clean sterilized glass bottle, seal and store in the refrigerator. Use within three weeks.

SPICED HAZELNUT COFFEE

SERVES 1 | GLASSWARE: COUPE GLASS

If you would like to take an after-dinner coffee to the next level of sophistication, with the flavours of sweet and woody cinnamon, earthy hazelnut and bold coffee, this cocktail might have been designed just for you. The combination of the shaken espresso and cream gives the serve a deliciously creamy texture and lovely layer of foam on top. To finish, the grated nutmeg provides an unbelievable aroma that is both warming and inviting.

INGREDIENTS
60 ml (2 fl oz) hazelnut or
   almond milk
15 ml (½ fl oz) Hazelnut Syrup
   (see below)
15 ml (½ fl oz) single (light) cream
Pinch of cinnamon
1 shot espresso
Grated nutmeg, to garnish

INSTRUCTIONS
Add the milk, hazelnut syrup, cream and a pinch of cinnamon to a shaker. Top with ice, add the espresso and shake well.

Double strain into a coupe glass and garnish with grated nutmeg.

HAZELNUT SYRUP
MAKES 300 ML (10 FL OZ)

INGREDIENTS
200 g (1 cup) granulated sugar
240 ml (8 fl oz) water
135g (1 cup) whole blanched
   hazelnuts

INSTRUCTIONS
Roughly chop the hazelnuts. Add the sugar, water and hazelnuts to a saucepan and bring to the boil. Reduce the heat and simmer, stirring, for 10 minutes until the sugar has dissolved. Remove from the heat and leave to infuse for 30 minutes. Strain into a glass jar, seal and store in the refrigerator. Use within four weeks.

SOBER IN MANHATTAN

SERVES 1 | GLASSWARE: COUPE GLASS

As the name suggests, this is a non-alcoholic twist on the popular classic cocktail known as the Manhattan. The original recipe was invented by Dr Iain Marshall in the early 1880s for a party being held by Lady Randolph Churchill, the mother of Winston Churchill. The serve has a slight bitterness and some herbal undertones from the bitters and vermouth, and the expressed orange oil gives the drink an intense bittersweet aroma.

INGREDIENTS

60 ml (2 fl oz) non-alcoholic malt spirit

30 ml (1 fl oz) non-alcoholic sweet vermouth

2 dashes aromatic bitters, such as Angostura

Orange peel

Maraschino cherry, to garnish

INSTRUCTIONS

Add the malt spirit, sweet vermouth and bitters to a mixing glass, top with ice cubes and stir for 45 seconds. Single strain into a coupe glass.

To express the oil from the orange peel, fold the peel in half with the white pith facing outwards and, holding it above the glass, squeeze on the fold to express the oil. You should see little droplets of oil released in a puffy cloud. Garnish with a maraschino cherry.

MARZIPAN SOUR

SERVES 1 | GLASSWARE: ROCKS (OLD-FASHIONED) GLASS

This sour is a based on the classic Amaretto Sour, which is thought to have been created in 1974 by Portland bartender Jeffrey Morgenthaler, the first US importer of Amaretto di Saronno, an almond liqueur that has been enjoyed in Italy since 1525. The almond flavour comes from the syrup, which, combined with the lemon juice and egg white, creates a cocktail with a silky texture.

INGREDIENTS

60 ml (2 fl oz) non-alcoholic malt spirit
30 ml (1 fl oz) freshly squeezed
   lemon juice
22.5 ml (¾ fl oz) Almond Syrup
   (see below)
1 egg white or 30 ml (1 fl oz) aquafaba
   (chickpea water)
2 dashes aromatic bitters, such as
   Angostura
Lemon peel strip, to garnish

INSTRUCTIONS

Add the malt spirit, lemon juice, almond syrup, egg white and aromatic bitters to a shaker and dry shake (without ice). Add ice and shake well again to chill.

   Double strain into a rocks glass filled with ice cubes and garnish with a twist of lemon peel.

ALMOND SYRUP

MAKES 350 ML (12 ½ FL OZ)

INGREDIENTS

200 g (1 cup) granulated sugar
240 ml (8 fl oz) water
140g (1 ¼ cup) whole almonds

INSTRUCTIONS

Pulse the almonds in a food processor until finely chopped. Add to a bowl with the water, cover and refrigerate for 8 hours. Strain into a saucepan, add the sugar and bring to the boil. Reduce to a simmer, and stir for 5 minutes, then cool for 30 minutes. Strain into a glass jar, seal and store in the refrigerator. Use within four weeks.

CARROT & GINGER SMASH

SERVES 1 | GLASSWARE: ROCKS (OLD-FASHIONED) GLASS

Carrot is not an ingredient often used in cocktails, but that should definitely change. With its vibrant, bright colour and sweet, earthy flavours, it has the perfect characteristics for a delicious cocktail. For this serve the carrot flavour is enhanced by the bittersweet orange liqueur, and the ginger syrup provides a sweet yet fiery finish. The mint sprig garnish adds a delightful fresh herbal nose.

INGREDIENTS
60 ml (2 fl oz) non-alcoholic
    orange liqueur
45 ml (1 ½ fl oz) carrot juice
15 ml (½ fl oz) Ginger Syrup
    (see below)
22.5 ml (¾ fl oz) freshly squeezed
    lime juice

GARNISH
Piece of crystallized ginger
Fresh mint sprig

INSTRUCTIONS
Add the orange liqueur, carrot juice, ginger syrup and lime juice to a cocktail shaker filled with ice and shake well. Add ice cubes to the rocks glass and double strain the cocktail mixture into it.

Garnish with a piece of crystallized ginger and mint sprig.

GINGER SYRUP
MAKES 350 ML (12 ½ FL OZ)

INGREDIENTS
200 g (1 cup) granulated sugar
240 ml (8 fl oz) water
100 g (1 cup) sliced fresh ginger
    (ginger root)
2 lemon peel strips

INSTRUCTIONS
Add the sugar and water to a saucepan and bring to the boil. Add the ginger and lemon and simmer for 10 minutes, stirring until the sugar is dissolved. Remove from the heat and leave to infuse for 1 hour. Strain into a clean sterilized glass bottle and store in the refrigerator. Use within three weeks.

SALTED TOFFEE APPLE

SERVES 2 | GLASSWARE: MARTINI GLASSES

Basically a dessert in a glass, this cocktail is perfect for those who love biting into a salted toffee apple. It combines apple juice, fresh lime juice and salted caramel sauce for a balance of sweet, sour and salty. The vanilla bitters add a hint of warmth in the background and help to enhance all the other flavours.

INGREDIENTS
120 ml (4 fl oz) apple juice
60 ml (2 fl oz) freshly squeezed
   lime juice
2 barspoons Salted Caramel Sauce
   (see below)
2 dashes vanilla bitters
2 apple fans, to garnish (see page 17)

FOR THE RIM
Lime wedge
Sea salt

INSTRUCTIONS
Coat the rim of each glass: wet half the rim using the lime wedge and roll in the sea salt.

Add the apple juice, lime juice, salted caramel sauce and vanilla bitters to a cocktail shaker filled with ice and shake well.

Double strain equally into the two prepared Martini glasses and garnish with apple fans.

SALTED CARAMEL SAUCE

INGREDIENTS
200 g (1 cup) granulated sugar
85 g (⅓ cup) salted butter
120 ml (½ cup) double (heavy) cream
1 tsp salt

INSTRUCTIONS
Add the granulated sugar to a saucepan over a medium heat. Stir continuously until the sugar breaks down into a smooth, amber-coloured liquid. Add the butter and keep stirring until combined. Slowly pour in the cream, stirring constantly. After 1 minute, stop stiring and the caramel will rise in the pan. Remove from the heat and stir in the salt.

Allow to slightly cool and pour into a glass jar, seal and store in the refrigerator. Use within four weeks.

ALMOND & CINNAMON FIZZ

SERVES 1 | GLASSWARE: HIGHBALL GLASS

Based on the classic Ramos Gin Fizz, a creamy, citrussy, fizzy serve, this non-alcoholic cocktail celebrates the flavours of almond and cinnamon by including the milk and syrup, which are combined with lemon juice for balance. The introduction of egg white provides the drink with a beautifully creamy texture, and as the soda is poured in, the foam rises above the rim to create the distinctive look of the fizz.

INGREDIENTS

45 ml (1 ½ fl oz) almond milk
15 ml (½ fl oz) Cinnamon Syrup
    (see page 86)
22.5 ml (¾ fl oz) freshly squeezed
    lemon juice
1 egg white or 30 ml (1 fl oz) aquafaba
    (chickpea water)
Soda water (club soda), to top
Ground cinnamon, to garnish

INSTRUCTIONS

Add the almond milk, cinnamon syrup, lemon juice and egg white to a cocktail shaker and dry shake (without ice).

Add ice to the shaker and shake again to chill. Double strain into a tall glass, let settle for 45 seconds, then pour in the soda water until the foam rises above the rim.

Garnish with a pinch of cinnamon and add a straw.

HOT TODDY

SERVES 1 | GLASSWARE: HEATPROOF ROCKS (OLD-FASHIONED) GLASS

The inspiration for this serve is the classic hot cocktail of the same name, the Hot Toddy. Its origins are unknown, but one story is that an Irish doctor named Robert Bentley Todd was said to have prescribed something similar to his patients. Whatever the cocktail's origin, this non-alcoholic version is a delicious mix of warming spices, citrussy lemon and sweet honey syrup, making it perfect for a chilly day in winter.

INGREDIENTS
22.5 ml (¾ fl oz) freshly squeezed
   lemon juice
15 ml (½ fl oz) Honey Syrup
   (see page 36)
Pinch of ground cinnamon
1 clove
1 star anise
Cinnamon stick, to garnish

INSTRUCTIONS
Add the lemon juice, honey syrup, pinch of cinnamon, clove and star anise to a hot drinks glass.

Top with boiling water and stir well. Garnish with a cinnamon stick.

WINTER TONIC

SERVES 1 | GLASSWARE: HIGHBALL GLASS

As the name suggests, this cocktail is one that is perfect for winter, but it's just as enjoyable in the other seasons. With the combination of the sweet, tart cranberry juice, citrussy lemon and warming, sweet ginger syrup, the serve has a complex, delicious flavour. The Indian tonic water adds a refreshing aspect, and the rosemary sprig gives it a subtle herbal flavour and a pleasant aroma.

INGREDIENTS
7.5 ml (¼ fl oz) Ginger Syrup
  (see page 126)
15 ml (½ fl oz) freshly squeezed
  lemon juice
45 ml (1 ½ fl oz) cranberry juice
45 ml (1 ½ fl oz) Indian tonic water
Fresh rosemary spring, to garnish

INSTRUCTIONS
Pour the ginger syrup, lemon juice, cranberry juice and Indian tonic water into a tall glass filled with ice cubes and stir with a barspoon to combine.
    Garnish with a rosemary sprig.

134

MULLED APPLE PARTY JUG

SERVES 10 | GLASSWARE: HEATPROOF JUG AND ROCKS (OLD-FASHIONED) GLASSES

Mulled cider was offered at a medieval English drinking ritual called wassailing, a ceremony to bless the apple trees for a bountiful harvest at Christmas time. This non-alcoholic version still pays homage to the key ingredient, the apple. The sweet, tart apple juice is infused with a combination of delicious spices and bittersweet orange, and the maple syrup brings it all together. Served warm, it is the perfect for celebrating the festive winter period.

INGREDIENTS
1.5 litre (3 pints) apple juice
3 sticks cinnamon
6 cloves
2 star anise
100 ml (3 ½ fl oz) maple syrup
1 vanilla pod
1 orange, juice and peel
4 lemon peel strips

GARNISH
10 apple slices
10 star anise

INSTRUCTIONS
Add all the ingredients to a saucepan, bring to the boil, then reduce to a medium-low heat. Simmer, stirring, for 5 minutes.

Remove from the heat and leave to infuse for 30 minutes.

Reheat to the desired temperature and transfer to a heatproof jug. Serve in heatproof glasses, each garnished with an apple slice and star anise.

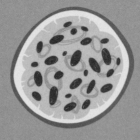

FAVOURITES

I don't have a single favourite cocktail, or even a certain type. You will see from the collection of cocktails included in this book that they're all very different and are great for different occasions. I like to choose the cocktail based on the event or meal, whether it is brunch or after dinner. I have included here some of my favourite cocktails to be enjoyed across the board, at any time of day. Many of these are twists on classics, such as the Espresso Martini and the Nuts & Berries, but there are also some originals. I hope you enjoy them as much as I do.

PASSION FRUIT MARTINI

SERVES 1 | GLASSWARE: COUPE GLASS AND SHOT GLASS

The popular Pornstar Martini was created by Douglas Ankrah (of the famous Lab Bar in London) after trying a drink at a 'louche gentlemen's club' called Mavericks while visiting Cape Town in South Africa. In this non-alcoholic version, pineapple and passion fruit are combined with vanilla to give the serve a sweet, tropical, slightly spiced finish. Taking a sip from the non-alcoholic sparkling wine first will cleanse the palate and make the next sip of the cocktail more intense.

INGREDIENTS

60 ml (2 fl oz) pineapple juice
30 ml (1 fl oz) passion fruit purée
1 barspoon Vanilla Syrup (see
    page 56)
15 ml (½ fl oz) freshly squeezed
    lime juice
1 shot non-alcoholic sparkling wine
½ passion fruit, to garnish

INSTRUCTIONS

Add the pineapple juice, passion fruit purée, vanilla syrup and lime juice to a cocktail shaker filled with ice and shake well.

Double strain into a coupe glass. Garnish with half a passion fruit and serve with a shot glass of non-alcoholic sparkling wine.

ESPRESSO MARTINI

SERVES 1 | GLASSWARE: COUPE GLASS

Here is a non-alcoholic twist on a modern-day classic: the Espresso Martini.
It was created by Dick Bradsell, a bartender who worked at Fred's Club, a bar
in London, in the 1980s. The story goes, a young (now famous) model walked
into the bar and asked for a drink that would wake them up, and that is how the
Espresso Martini was born. With the combination of bitter coffee balanced by
sweetness, it is the perfect dessert cocktail.

INGREDIENTS

30 ml (1 fl oz) non-alcoholic
   coffee liqueur
30 ml (1 fl oz) non-alcoholic white
   cane spirit
7.5 ml (¼ fl oz) Vanilla Syrup
   (see page 56)
1 shot espresso
3 coffee beans, to garnish

INSTRUCTIONS

Add the coffee liqueur, white cane
spirit and vanilla syrup to a cocktail
shaker, fill with ice and pour in the
espresso. Shake well, then double
strain into a coupe glass.
   Garnish with the coffee beans.

Tip: When adding hot ingredients to
your cocktail shaker glass, add the ice
before the hot ingredients to prevent
the glass from cracking.

NUTS & BERRIES

SERVES 1 | GLASSWARE: ROCKS (OLD-FASHIONED) GLASS

The name of this drink describes exactly what you'll get. It's based on the classic going by the same name, which is a combination of vodka, cream and hazelnut and berry liqueurs. This non-alcoholic version has all the classic flavours but in a more natural way, with the fresh muddled raspberries and homemade blackberry syrup. The hazelnut milk adds a subtle nut flavour, with the chopped almonds on the rim taking it up a notch.

INGREDIENTS

3 raspberries
15 ml (1 fl oz) Blackberry Syrup
  (see below)
60 ml (2 fl oz) hazelnut milk
30 ml (1 fl oz) single (light) cream
3 raspberries, to garnish

FOR THE RIM

Blackberry Syrup (see below)
Finely chopped roasted hazelnuts

INSTRUCTIONS

Coat the rim of the glass: wet half the rim with blackberry syrup and roll it in the roasted hazelnuts.

Add the raspberries to a cocktail shaker, pour in the blackberry syrup and muddle.

Add the hazelnut milk and single cream, top with ice cubes and shake.

Add ice cubes to the prepared glass and double strain the cocktail into it.

Garnish with raspberries.

BLACKBERRY SYRUP
MAKES 350 ML (12½ FL OZ)

INGREDIENTS

300 g (2 cups) blackberries
200 g (1 cup) granulated sugar
240 ml (8 fl oz) water
2 lemon peel strips

INSTRUCTIONS

Add all the ingredients to a saucepan and bring to the boil. Reduce to a simmer for 5 minutes, stirring until the sugar has dissolved. Remove from the heat and leave to cool. Strain into a clean sterilized glass bottle and store in the refrigerator. Use within two weeks.

VIRGIN MARY

SERVES 1 | GLASSWARE: HIGHBALL GLASS

A classic vodka cocktail, the Bloody Mary, is behind this creation. The original version most likely came about in the 1920s at Harry's New York Bar in Paris. At the time Russians were emigrating to Paris and brought vodka along with them. Bartender Ferdinand Petiot found the spirit tasteless and began experimenting. After many failed cocktails, he combined it with tomato juice and seasoning, and the Bloody Mary was born. This non-alcoholic version has all the beautiful flavours of the classic, but without the 'tasteless' vodka.

INGREDIENTS

90 ml (3 fl oz) tomato juice

15 ml (½ fl oz) freshly squeezed lemon juice

2 dashes Worcestershire sauce

2 dashes hot chilli sauce, such as Tabasco (more if you like it spicy)

Pinch of celery salt

FOR THE RIM

Lemon wedge

Celery salt

GARNISH

Celery stick

Gherkin

Lemon wedge

INSTRUCTIONS

Coat the rim of the glass: wet half the rim using the lemon wedge and roll it in the celery salt.

Add the tomato juice, lemon juice, Worcestershire sauce, hot chilli sauce and a pinch of celery salt to a tall glass filled with cubed ice. Stir with a barspoon for 30 seconds to chill the cocktail and combine the ingredients.

Garnish with a celery stick, gherkin and lemon wedge.

CHOCOLATE ORANGE COFFEE MARTINI

SERVES 1 | GLASSWARE: COUPE GLASS

The bittersweet orange liqueur combined with the sweet chocolate syrup in this cocktail creates a flavour any chocolatier would be proud of. Adding the coffee liqueur and espresso takes the drink to the next level, creating a beautiful foam.

INGREDIENTS
30 ml (1 fl oz) each of non-alcoholic orange liqueur and non-alcoholic coffee liqueur
15 ml (½ fl oz) Chocolate Syrup (see below)
1 shot espresso
Grated orange chocolate, to garnish

INSTRUCTIONS
Add the coffee liqueur, orange liqueur and chocolate sauce to a cocktail shaker, fill with ice and pour in the espresso. Shake well, then double strain into a coupe glass.

Serve garnished with the grated chocolate on top.

CHOCOLATE SYRUP

INGREDIENTS
170 g (1 cup) dark chocolate chips
125 ml (½ cup) double (heavy) cream
30 g (2 tbsp) unsalted butter
Pinch of salt
1 tbsp brown sugar

INSTRUCTIONS
Add all the ingredients to a glass bowl and microwave for 60 seconds. Remove and cover with a plate for 10 minutes. Then gently whisk until combined and smooth. Pour into a glass jar, seal and store in the refrigerator. Use within four weeks.

STRAWBERRY & LEMON MERINGUE

SERVES 1 | GLASSWARE: COUPE GLASS

The popular tangy, sweet and cloud-like meringue is the perfect inspiration for a cocktail. Here strawberries and lemon work together to create a clean fruity drink that is not only a great dessert cocktail but also one that can be enjoyed anytime. The egg white helps to combine the ingredients and creates a delicious creamy texture. Torching the top of the cocktail produces an incredible aroma and pays homage to the classic dessert, which is often caramelized when served.

INGREDIENTS

2 strawberries, halved

15 ml (½ fl oz) Simple Syrup (see page 32)

60 ml (2 fl oz) cloudy lemonade, allowed to go flat

15 ml (½ fl oz) freshly squeezed lemon juice

1 egg white or 30 ml (1 fl oz) aquafaba (chickpea water)

½ strawberry, to garnish

INSTRUCTIONS

Add the strawberries and simple syrup to a cocktail shaker and muddle. Pour in the cloudy lemonade, lemon juice and egg white, then dry shake (without ice). Add ice and shake again to chill.

Double strain into a coupe glass. Caramelize the top of the cocktail using a kitchen blowtorch and garnish with the strawberry.

RESOURCES & SUPPLIERS

I've compiled my tried-and-tested zero-proof brands here, as well as mixers for cocktail-making. These brands deliver spirits with flavour profiles that mimic their alcoholic counterparts best. For the recipes in this book, I tend to use the following brands, but feel free to explore the ranges each one has to offer and those that are available near you.

Sparkling cocktails: Freixenet and Wild Life Botanicals for the zero-proof alternative to prosecco and Champagne.
Botanical cocktails: Seedlip, Pentire, Clean Co. and Tanquery have fabulous gin alternatives.
Tropical cocktails: Zero-proof brands that are labelled sugar cane or tropical can be used interchangeably for a rum flavour profile. My favourites are from Caleño and Lyre.
Agave cocktails: For a tequila subsitute, choose from Lyre's agave blanco and Clean Co.'s Clean T oaky agave.
Bittersweet cocktails: For Campari- and Aperol-style flavours, choose APRTF bitter aperitif, Lyre's Italian orange, Tuscan Tree's blood orange aperitivo or Wilfred's apertif.
Dark and spicy cocktails: Try Lyre's American Malt or the US brand Spiritless – Kentucky 74 or Kentucky 74 Spiced – for whisky flavours.

APRTF BITTER APERITIF
innathome.co.uk/aprtf-bitter-aperitif-0
A range of familiar flavours for the mindful drinker, APRTF was started by two friends and uses a non-alcoholic distillery in Monmouth, Wales. The beautifully balanced bitter aperitif is the perfect mixer for a Negroni-style drink.

BUNDABERG BREWED DRINKS
bundaberg.com
Carefully crafted soft drinks from a small, family-owned Australian brand. Offering a select range of beers, Bundaberg is best known for its craft brewed ginger beer, made from quality local ingredients.

CALEÑO DRINKS
calenodrinks.com
A distilled, light and zesty blend of tropical, citrus and spice botanical spirits. Along with tropical spirits, Caleño sell cases of tropical pre-mixed cocktail cans, taster boxes and bundles, perfect for mixing your own drink.

CLEAN CO.
clean.co
Selling a range of non-alcoholic alternatives, with a focus on replicating the taste and mouthfeel of alcohol, the brand was founded by British reality TV personality Spencer Matthews. Specialties include gin, rum and tequila alternatives.

CROSSIP

crossipdrinks.com

Texture, depth and mouthfeel are the focus for the UK company Crossip in creating a sophisticated NA drink. They use a core base of eucalyptus, ginger, cayenne, centian and vegetable glycerin. Their Blazing Pineapple is perfect for tropical cocktails while Dandy Smoke is great for an espresso martini or whisky sour alternative.

DOUBLE DUTCH

doubledutchdrinks.com

Carefully crafted premium drinking mixers and tonics. Along with its flavoured mixers, sodas and lemonades, Double Dutch is best known for its award-winning Indian tonic water with hints of pink grapefruit and juniper berry.

DRINK MONDAY

drinkmonday.co

Award-winning Californian producers of zero-proof rum, whiskey, mezcal and gin, as well as cocktail kits, their tagline is 'free of alcohol, full of spirit'.

FEVER-TREE

fever-tree.com

High-quality tonic water, mixers and sodas, including gingers and lemonades. Focused on the tonic that makes up three-quarters of your drink, Fever-tree's speciality lies in their award-winning tonic water, individually crafted to complement the varied flavour profiles of every drink.

FREE SPIRITS

drinkfreespirits.com

Free Spirits was created to enable people to enjoy their favourite cocktails while controlling the amount of alcohol that's used in the creation, all without sacrificing taste. The Californian brand uses a method they call 'distillate reconstruction' to produce the alchemy of the flavour profiles for bourbon, gin, tequila and aperitivo.

FREIXENET

freixenet.com

Beautifully aged alcohol-free wines from the world-renown Catalan family-owned vitners. Selling a variety of NA wines, their specialties include prosecco, rosé and white wine.

GNISTA

gnistaspirits.com

Offering complexity, body and big flavour, this Swedish brand produces 'not wine', developed and approved by sommeliers, as well as spirits with botanical names such as Floral Wormwood and Barreled Oak.

KIN EUPHORICS

kineuphorics.com

Co-founded by model Bella Hadid, this producer of non-alcoholic, benefit-driven, alternative drinks and spirits includes made-to-mix spirits filled with adaptogens, nootropics and botanicals, infused drinks, as well as variety packs and kits for you to mix your own cocktails.

LYRE'S SPIRIT CO.

lyres.co.uk

Carefully crafted non-alcoholic spirits from a boutique British brand. Along with gin, bourbon, agave and rum (spiced cane) substitutes, there are set mixes to make up Espresso Martinis, Porn Star Martinis and Jungle Birds and premixed drinks. Specialities include coffee liqueur, orange liqueur, Italian aperitivo and red vermouth.

MINGLE MOCKTAILS

minglemocktails.com

Naturally infused botanical beverages. Recreating favourite cocktail flavours, the company produces a range of fruity non-alcoholic alternatives to margaritas, mimosas, Bellinis and more. Each is available in a bottle, can or customizable variety pack.

MONIN

monin.com

Best known for their gourmet flavoured syrups, from simple sugar syrup to the zesty blue Curaçao, Monin also carries a variety of organic sweeteners, cocktail mixers, purées and ready-made mixes.

PENTIRE DRINKS

pentiredrinks.com

Plant-based non-alcoholic spirits from a boutique Cornish brand. Selling a range of botanical alcohol-free spirits, Pentire is best known for their gin-style drinks that focus on herby, bitter and refreshing tones with coastal-inspired names such as Adrift and Seaward. There are also tonic waters and pre-mixed non-alcoholic cocktails.

REMEDY DRINKS

remedydrinks.com

A variety of non-alcoholic drinks with a focus on health benefits. Alongside soft drinks, energizers, shots and ACV drinks, Remedy is known for its wide range of fruity, citrus kombuchas. Each can be purchased in a mixed sample pack or case.

RITUAL ZERO PROOF

ritualzeroproof.com

Founded by friends with the goal to add a new tool to the cocktail kit rather than replace liquor entirely, the Chicago-based company produces gin, rum, whiskey and aperitivo alternatives.

SEEDLIP

seedlipdrinks.com

One of the first distilled alcohol-free spirit brands, this boutique British company focuses on warm, aromatic and zesty flavours and complex blends, including the citrus Grove 42, the aromatic Spice 94 and the botanical Garden 108.

SEXY AF

sexyafspirits.com

Canadian company Sexy AF Spirits produce alcohol-free, plant-based, low-calorie, botanically infused spirits with names such as Friski Whiski, ViirGiin, Spiced Yum and Triple Sexy.

SPIRITLESS

spiritless.com

With whiskey, tequila and pour-over, ready-made classic cocktails, the US-based, female-founded brand serves up vegan and gluten-free zero-proof drinks. Their Kentucky 74 bourbon is underpinned by the familiar notes of caramel, vanilla and oak.

STRYKK

strykk.com

Launched with a range of 'Not' drinks, such as Not V*dka, Strykk spirits had to taste, look and feel as close to their alcoholic equivalents as possible. They are low in calories, ultra-low in carbs, with no sugar, no artificial flavours and zero alcohol.

TANQUERAY

tanqueray.com

From the company behind the famous London Dry and Flor De Sevilla gins comes a non-alcoholic version, Tanquerary 0.0%. It has a complex citrus and juniper-led profile.

THREE SPIRIT

threespiritdrinks.com

Celebrating what goes into a drink rather than what is taken out, Three Spirits NA drinks blend adaptogens, nootropics, herbs, distillates and ferments with specific mood-making benefits. The Livener is 'primed, fiery and energized' while the Nightcap is 'calming, woody and mellow'.

TUSCAN TREE

tuscan-tree.com

Full-bodied, classic Italian-style aperitivo spirits. Drawing inspiration from the Italian culture of 'aperitivo hour', Tuscan Tree offers a small range of beautifully balanced non-alcoholic alternatives, such as the 19-ingredient blood orange variety and cloudy elderflower. They make a perfect base for a wide range of mocktails and Negroni-style drinks.

WILD LIFE BOTANICALS

wildlifebotanicals.co.uk

An innovative approach on ultra-low and alcohol-free sparkling wine for conscious drinkers. Selling a carefully curated selection of wines, this Cornwall-based brand offers a range of bottles and cans, ideal for those on the go.

WILFRED'S APERITIF

wilfredsdrinks.com

A blend of natural botanicals for a new era of drinkers, the company was born from a quest for a spritz that had all the complexity of the greats but none of the alcohol. Wilfred's sells a full-bodied bittersweet orange and rosemary aperitif that's perfect for the brand's special: Wilfred's Negroni sbagliato.

INDEX

ACKNOWLEDGEMENTS

I would firstly like to give a special thanks to my wife, Mari. Without your love and support none of this would have been possible. Your positivity and encouragement drives me forward and allows me to be the best version of myself, and you were an incredible product tester when trying out the cocktail recipes. I would also like to acknowledge my children, Tomi and Lidia. You are my inspiration; my whole life ambition is to make you proud.

The completion of this book could not have been possible without the guidance and expertise of Lisa Dyer and the rest of the team at the Welbeck Publishing Group.

Finally I would like to thank Menna, Glyn and Gareth, the co-owners of Baravin in Aberystwyth, who employed me to manage the bar for six years. They gave me free rein and confidence to be creative: it's where I first fell in love with creating cocktails.